KNITS
for babies and toddlers

KNITS
for babies and toddlers

NEW HOLLAND

Fiona McTague

For Lucy and Molly

First published in 2001 by
New Holland Publishers (UK) Ltd
London • Cape Town • Sydney • Auckland

Garfield House
86-88 Edgware Road
London W2 2EA
United Kingdom

80 McKenzie Street
Cape Town 8001
South Africa

Level 1, Unit 4, 14 Aquatic Drive
Frenchs Forest, NSW 2086
Australia

218 Lake Road
Northcote, Auckland
New Zealand

2 4 6 8 10 9 7 5 3 1

ISBN 1 85974 624 1 (hb)
ISBN 1 85974 921 6 (pb)

Designer and art director: Frances de Rees
Pattern checker: Sue Whiting
Photographer: John Freeman
Diagrams: Carrie Hill
Illustrations: Moira McTague
Production: Caroline Hansell

Editorial Direction: Rosemary Wilkinson

Reproduction by PICA Colour Separation, Singapore
Printed and bound in Singapore by Tien Wah Press

CONTENTS

INTRODUCTION 6

TECHNIQUES

BASIC STITCHES 10

BASIC FABRICS 15

EMBROIDERY STITCHES 18

PATTERNS

JACKET, TROUSERS, SHORTS AND SHOES 22

SHORT BOLERO JACKET 28

THREE-IN-ONE GUERNSEYS 32

HOUSE, HEART AND FLOWER JACKET AND HAT 36

GARTER STITCH STRIPED JUMPER, HAT AND BOOTIES 40

EMBROIDERED MOSS STITCH JACKET AND BOOTIES 44

BODYWARMER 48

JACKET WITH LACE EDGING 52

STRIPED ROMPER SUIT 56

PICOT EDGE CARDIGAN AND BOOTIES 60

FAIR ISLE JACKET 64

FAIR ISLE TWINSET 68

HOODED MOSS STITCH JACKET 72

STRIPED TUNIC 76

SAMPLER SWEATER 80

MOSS STITCH CARDIGAN WITH CABLE EDGING 84

NAUTICAL JACKET AND SOCKS 88

SCANDINAVIAN JACKET AND HAT 92

WRAP-OVER TOP 96

HEART, STAR AND MOON BLANKET 100

LACY SHAWL 104

TOY DOG 108

STRIPED BAG AND HAT 112

BABY BLANKET 116

RABBIT FAMILY 120

SUPPLIERS, ACKNOWLEDGEMENTS AND INDEX 128

INTRODUCTION

Every new baby and young child is unique and I have designed this range of patterns with their individuality in mind. I hope that the projects will be enjoyable to create, a pleasure to give and special to receive. Perhaps the gift will become a treasured heirloom for future generations of your family. The 'Rabbit Family' toys, knitted to greet a new arrival, should continue to appeal to all age groups; the 'Wrap-over top' or 'Lacy shawl' would be perfect to mark a special occasion, such as a Christening.

The varied designs featured range from simple and easy to knit designs for the complete beginner to more challenging creations for the more experienced knitter. The patterns for the 'Garter stitch striped jumper, hat and booties' are ideal for the novice, whilst the intricate 'Fair Isle twinset' in 4 ply will appeal to even the most skilled.

Each project has straightforward, yet detailed instructions, charts where necessary and full-colour photographs showing the finished products. There is a full

back-up section supplying information on basic knitting techniques included for the absolute beginner. The experienced knitter can personalize the designs to create a more individual look.

The styles range from the most simple stripes and textured stitches to lace, Fair Isle, and multicoloured jacquard. All designs have an actual measurement included in the patterns, so readers can choose the size they prefer. With children in mind, the designs are practical, comfortable and wearable. A wide variety of natural and fine quality yarns have been selected, including cotton, pure wools and cashmere, featuring a wonderful palette from pastels to vibrant colours.

There are over 25 designs to choose from, covering a whole wardrobe of clothes as well as items for the nursery, such as blankets and toys. I really enjoyed designing each project and hope you will share my inspiration. Happy knitting.

TECHNIQUES

BEFORE CASTING ON

Before you begin
Before casting on you must get used to holding the yarn and the needles, this is very important as it controls the tension of the finished fabric.

Holding the yarn
Hold the yarn in the left hand, pass it under the little finger of the other hand, then around the same finger, over the third finger, under the second finger and over the index finger. The index finger is used to wind the yarn round the tip of the needle. The yarn wound round the little finger controls the tension of the yarn.

Holding the needles
Hold the right needle in the same position as a pencil. For casting on and the first few rows the knitting passes between the thumb and index finger. As the knitting grows, place the thumb under the knitting, holding the needle from below.

The left needle is held lightly over the top using the thumb and index finger to control the tip.

There are many ways of casting on, but the cable method is the one most commonly used.

Left-handed knitters
Knitting right handed can be confusing for left-handed people. To follow the instructions for casting on prop the book in front of a mirror and follow the diagrams in the mirror image. The yarn will then be controlled by the left hand.

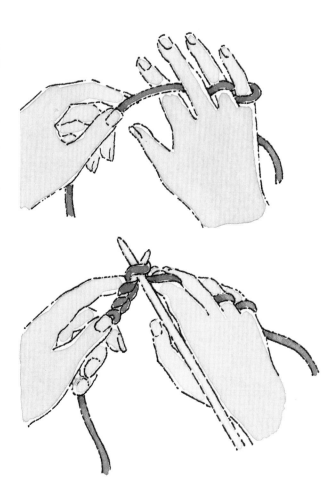

CASTING ON

This method of casting on gives a neat firm edge with a cable appearance.

1 Make a slip knot near the end of the yarn and place it on the left-hand needle.

2 Holding the yarn at the back of the needles, insert the tip of the right-hand needle into the loop, pass the yarn round the tip of the right needle.

3 Draw the right-hand needle through the slip knot, forming a loop on the right-hand needle, leave the slip knot on the left-hand needle.

4 Transfer the new loop on to the left-hand needle, there are now two stitches on the left-hand needle.

5 Insert the right-hand needle between the two stitches on the left-hand needle, wind the yarn round the point of the right-hand needle.

6 Draw a loop through and place it on the left-hand needle.
   Repeat steps 5 and 6 until you have the required number of stitches.

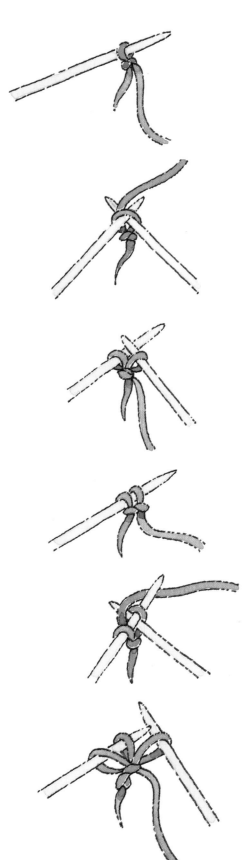

9

BASIC STITCHES

All knitting stitches, even the most complicated, are made from either knitting or purling.

How to knit

1 Hold the needle with the cast-on stitches in your left hand. With the yarn at the back of the work insert the right-hand needle, from front to back through the first stitch on the left-hand needle.

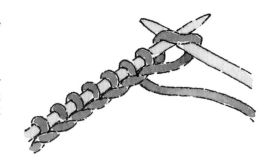

2 Wind the yarn from left to right over the top of the right-hand needle.

3 Draw the yarn through the stitch on the left-hand needle, making a new stitch on the right-hand needle.

4 Slip the original stitch off the left-hand needle.

To knit a row, repeat steps 1 to 4 until all the stitches have been transferred from the left-hand needle to the right-hand needle.

Turn the work and transfer the needle with the stitches on to the left hand to work the next row.

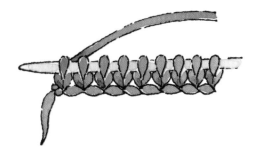

How to purl

1 Hold the needle containing the cast-on stitches in your left hand. With the yarn at the front of the work insert the right-hand needle, through the front of the first stitch on the left-hand needle, from right to left.

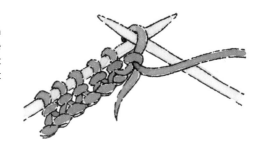

2 Wind the yarn from right to left over the point of the right-hand needle.

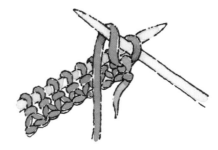

3 Draw the yarn through the stitch on the left-hand needle, making a new stitch on the right-hand needle.

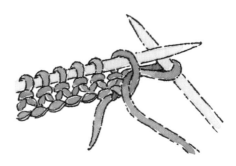

4 Slip the original stitch off the left-hand needle.

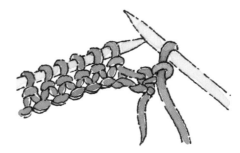

To purl a row, repeat steps 1 to 4 until all the stitches have been transferred from the left-hand needle to the right-hand needle.

Turn the work and transfer the needle with the stitches on to the left hand to work the next row.

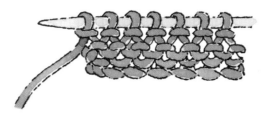

CASTING OFF

Casting off should be done in the same stitch at the same tension as the knitting, if it is too tight it will pucker, so try using a larger needle.

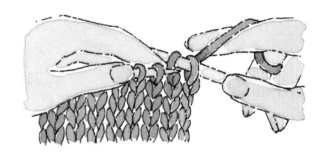

1 Knit the first two stitches in the usual way, so that both the stitches are on the right-hand needle.

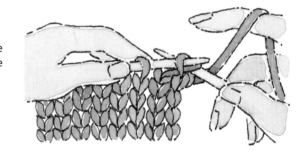

2 Using the point of the left-hand needle, lift the first knitted stitch over the second stitch and off the right-hand needle.

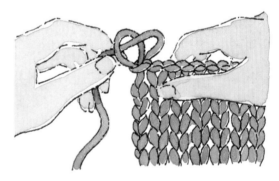

3 Knit another stitch onto the right-hand needle, then repeat from step 2 until one stitch remains. Leaving a long length for seaming, lengthen the stitch, then pull the end through the stitch to tighten it.

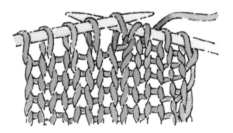

INCREASING

Increasing, by any one of a number of methods, is used to shape the fabric, making it wider.

Knitting into the same stitch twice (inc)

On a knit row, knit first into the front of the stitch then into the back of the stitch, before slipping off the original stitch. This makes two stitches from one. On a purl row, purl first into the front of the stitch then into the back of the stitch.

Invisible increasing

Before working the stitch on the needle, knit into the stitch below the one on the needle, then into the stitch on the needle. This method can also be used on a purl row.

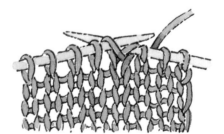

Raised increasing (m1)

Using the right-hand needle, pick up the bar that lies between the stitch just worked on the right-hand needle and the next stitch on the left-hand needle, place the bar on the left-hand needle, twisting it as you do so and knit into the back of it.

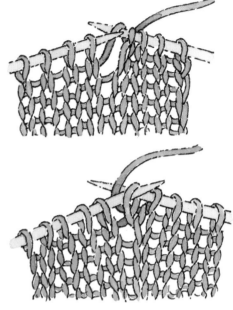

Making a stitch between two knit stitches (yfwd)

Bring the the yarn to the front between the needles, then take over the right-hand needle before knitting the next stitch.

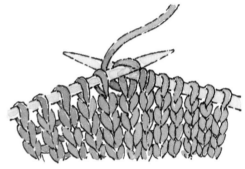

Making a stitch between two purl stitches (yrn)

Take the yarn over the right-hand needle to the back of the work, then bring the yarn to the front between the needles.

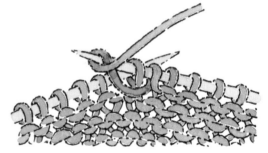

Making a stitch between a knit and a purl stitch (yon)

Having worked a knit stitch, bring the yarn forward under the right-hand needle, then wind it over the needle and back to the front. Purl the next stitch.

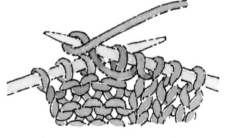

Extending a row

Cast on the required number of stitches at the beginning or end of the row, using the usual method.

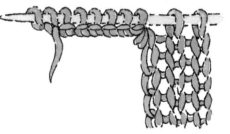

13

DECREASING

Decreasing, by any one of a number of methods, is used to reduce the number of stitches, making the fabric narrower.

Basic decreasing (k2tog)

This is the simplest and most commonly used method. Insert the right-hand needle from left to right through the second then the first stitch on the left-hand needle, knit the two stitches together, making one.

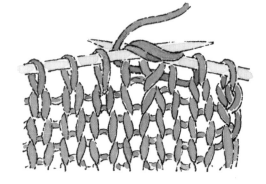

Purl decreasing (p2tog)

Insert the right-hand needle from right to left through the first two stitches on the left-hand needle, purl the two stitches together, making one stitch.

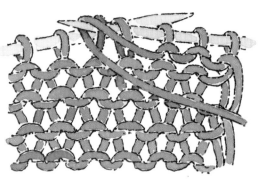

Slip stitch decreasing (skpo)

Slip a stitch from the left-hand needle onto the right-hand needle, knit the next stitch then, using the tip of the left needle, pass the slipped stitch over the last stitch on the right-hand needle and off the needle.

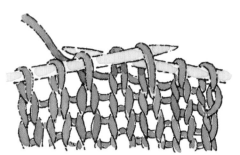

BASIC FABRICS

All knitted fabrics are made using just two basic stitches, knit and purl.

Garter stitch (g st) is often referred to as plain knitting because every row is made with the same stitch, either knit or purl. This produces a reversible fabric with raised horizontal ridges on both sides of the work. It is looser than stocking stitch. One of the advantages of garter stitch is that it does not curl so it can be used on its own, or for bands and borders.

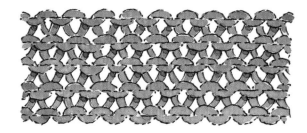

Stocking stitch (st st) is the most widely used knitted fabric. Alternate rows are knitted, the rest are purled. With the knit side as the right side it makes a flat, smooth surface that tends to curl at the edges. It needs finishing with bands, borders or hems where there would otherwise be a raw edge.

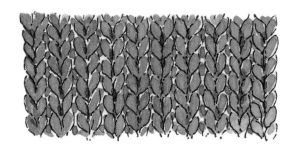

Single rib is formed by alternating knit and purl stitches on each row to form columns of stitches. It produces a very elastic fabric which is ideal for welts, neckbands and borders. It is generally knitted on a smaller needle than the main fabric to keep it firm and elastic.

For an even number of stitches the pattern will be as follows:
*k1, p1, rep from * to end

1 Knit the first stitch.

2 Bring the yarn through the needles to the front of the work and purl the next stitch.

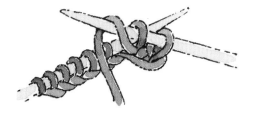

3 Take the yarn through the needles to the back of the work and knit the next stitch.
    Repeat steps 2 and 3 until all the stitches are on the right needle, ending with a purl stitch.
    Turn the work and start again from step 1.

Moss stitch is a basic textured stitch. It is made up of alternating knit and purl stitches. Stitches that are knitted on one row will be knitted on the next row and stitches that are purled on one row will be purled on the following row. If an odd number of stitches is cast on, every row will begin and end with a knit stitch. The fabric is firm, non curling and reversible, making it ideal for collars and cuffs.

For an odd number of stitches, the instructions will be as follows:

Patt row: K1, * p1, k1, rep from * to end.
Repeat this row.

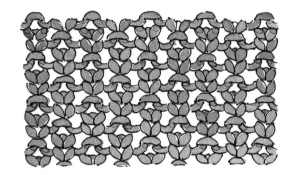

CABLES

Cables are usually worked in a stocking stitch column on a reversed stocking stitch background. Cables can be worked over any number of even stitches. The more stitches in the cable, the more rows that are worked between the cable twists.

How to make a cable 6 back

The following instructions are for a 6-stitch cable, but the same principle works for any size cable. The cable will curve to the right.

1 On the right side row, work to the position of the cable panel. Slip the next three stitches onto a cable needle and leave at the back of work. Knit the next three stitches in the usual way.

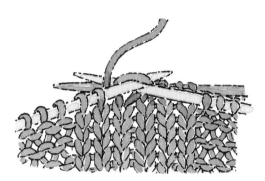

2 Now knit the three stitches from the cable needle, this completes the cable twist.

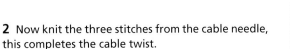

How to make a cable 6 front

The following instructions are for a 6-stitch cable, but the same principle works for any size cable. The cable will curve to the left.

1 On the right side row, work to the position of the cable panel. Slip the next three stitches onto a cable needle and leave at the front of work. Knit the next three stitches in the usual way.

2 Now knit the three stitches from the cable needle, this completes the cable twist.

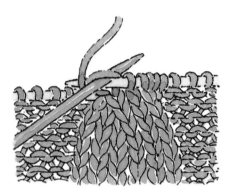

BASIC INFORMATION

TENSION

Obtaining the correct tension/gauge is extremely important. It controls both the shape and size of an article, so any variations, however slight, can distort the finished look of the garment. We strongly advise that you knit a square in pattern and/or stocking stitch (depending on the pattern instruction) of perhaps 5 – 10 more stitches and 5 – 10 more rows than those given in the tension note. Place the finished square on a flat surface and measure the central area.

If you have too many stitches to 10 cm try again using thicker needles, if you have too few stitches to 10 cm try again using finer needles. Once you have achieved the correct tension your garment will be knitted to the measurements given at the beginning of each pattern.

SIZE NOTE

The instructions are given for the smallest size. Where they vary, work the figures in brackets for the larger sizes. One set of figures refers to all sizes.

CHART NOTE

Some of the patterns in the book are worked from charts. Each square on a chart represents a stitch and each line of squares a row of knitting. When working from the charts, read odd rows (K) from right to left and the even rows (P) from left to right, unless otherwise stated. Each colour used is given a different symbol or letter and these are shown in the materials section, or in the key alongside the chart of each pattern.

KNITTING WITH COLOUR

There are two main methods of working colour into a knitted fabric: intarsia and Fair Isle techniques. The first method produces a single thickness of fabric and is usually used where a colour is only required in a particular area of a row and does not form a repeating pattern across the row.

Intarsia:

The simplest way to do this is to cut short lengths of yarn for each motif or block of colour used in a row. Then joining in the various colours at the appropriate point on the row, link one colour to the next by twisting them around each other where they meet on the wrong side to avoid gaps. All ends can then either be darned along the colour join lines, as each motif is completed, or can be "knitted-in" to the fabric of the knitting as each colour is worked into the pattern. This is done in much the same way as "weaving-in" yarns for the Fair Isle technique and does save time darning-in ends. It is essential that the tension is noted for intarsia as this may vary from the stocking stitch if both are used in the same pattern.

Fair Isle type knitting:

When two or three colours are worked repeatedly across a row, strand the yarn not in use loosely behind the stitches being worked. If you are working with more than two colours, treat the "floating" yarns as if they were one yarn and always spread the stitches to their correct width to keep them elastic. It is advisable not to carry the stranded or "floating" yarns over more than three stitches at a time, but to weave them under and over the colour you are working. The "floating" yarns are therefore caught at the back of the work.

PRESSING

After working for hours knitting a garment, it is worthwhile taking extra time and care on pressing and finishing it. After darning in all the ends, block each piece, except ribs, gently, using a warm iron over a damp cloth. Take special care to press the edges as this will make the sewing up both easier and neater. After sewing up, press seams and hems. Ribbed welts and neckbands and any areas of garter stitch should not be pressed.

FINISHING INSTRUCTIONS

When stitching the pieces together, match the colour patterns very carefully. Use a back stitch for all main knitting seams and an edge to edge stitch for all ribs unless otherwise stated. Join left shoulder seam using a back stitch and neckband seam (where appropriate) using an edge to edge stitch.

Sleeves and pockets

Set in sleeves: Set in sleeves easing sleeve head into armhole using a back stitch.

Square set in sleeves: Set in sleeve head into armhole, the straight sides at top of sleeve to form a neat right-angle to cast off sts at armhole on back and front, using back stitch.

Straight cast off sleeve: Place centre of cast off edge of sleeve to shoulder seam.

Sew in sleeve using back stitch using markers as guidelines where applicable. Join side and sleeve seams using a back stitch.

Slip stitch pocket edgings and linings into place. Sew on buttons.

EMBROIDERY STITCHES

Bullion stitch

Bring needle out at A. Insert at B and emerge at A, leaving needle in fabric. Wind yarn around needle eight times then pull it out carefully. Insert needle back at B, pulling yarn tightly.

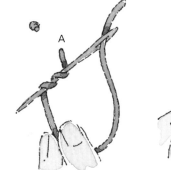
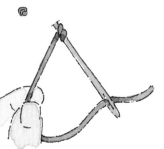
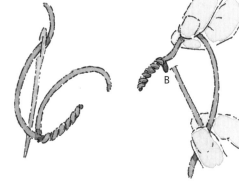

French knot

Bring needle out at A. Wind yarn round it twice. Turn, pulling twists lightly against needle. Insert back immediately next to the hole from which it emerged. Pull yarn through to back.

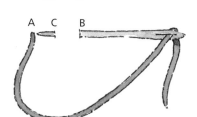
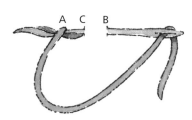

Stem stitch

Bring needle out at A. Insert back at B and emerge at C [half way between A and B].

Lazy daisy stitch embroidery is added to create an individual look on this smart jacket.

Lazy daisy stitch

Bring needle out at A. Insert back at A, and emerge at B, looping yarn under tip of needle. Pull needle through and over loop and insert at C. Emerge at D for next stitch.

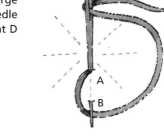
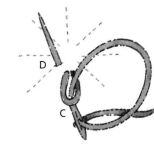

Star stitch

Bring needle out at A, insert at B, and emerge at C. Insert needle at D, emerge at E, insert needle at F, thus completing the stitch.

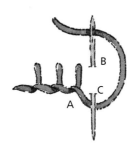
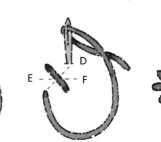

Blanket stitch

Bring needle out at A. Work from left to right. Insert needle at B and emerge at C. Wind yarn under point of needle and pull needle out. Repeat along the edge, making all the stitches the same height.

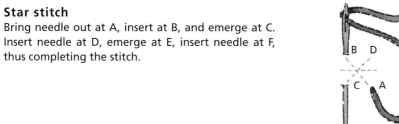

KNITTING NEEDLE CONVERSION TABLE

Metric	British	American
2 mm	14	00
2¼ mm	13	0
2¾ mm	12	2
3 mm	11	2/3
3¼ mm	10	3
3¾ mm	9	5
4 mm	8	6
4½ mm	7	7
5 mm	6	8
5½ mm	5	8
6 mm	4	9
6½ mm	3	10
7 mm	2	10½
7½ mm	1	11
8 mm	0	12
9 mm	00	13
10 mm	000	15

GLOSSARY OF UK/US TERMS

cast off = bind off; colour = shade; tension = gauge; knit up = pick up and knit; make up (garment) = finish (garment); moss stitch = seed stitch; st st = stockinette st; yarn forward, yarn over needle or yarn round needle = yarn over.

ABBREVIATIONS

alt	alternate
beg	begin(ning)
cont	continue
cm	centimetres
dec	decreas(e)(ing)
foll	following
g st	garter stitch (k every row)
inc	increas(e)(ing)
k	knit
m1	make one by raised increasing
mm	millimetres
meas	measures
patt	pattern
p	purl
psso	pass slipped stitch over
rem	remain(ing)
rep	repeat
rev st st	reverse stocking stitch (RS row p, WS row k)
RS	right side
skpo	slip 1, knit 1, pass slipped stitch over
sl 1	slip one stitch
st(s)	stitch(es)
st st	stocking stitch (RS row k, WS row p)
tbl	through back of loop(s)
tog	together
WS	wrong side
yb	yarn back
yfwd	yarn forward
yon	yarn over needle
yrn	yarn round needle

CARE INSTRUCTIONS
Check on ball band for washing instructions.

YARNS
Rowan Cotton Glace: a lightweight cotton yarn (100% cotton); approximately 115 m/125 yd per 50 g/1³/₄ oz ball.

Rowan Designer DK: a double knitting-weight yarn (100%pure new wool); approximately 115 m/125 yd per 50 g/1³/₄ oz ball.

Rowan Handknit DK Cotton: a medium-weight cotton yarn (100% cotton); approximately 85 m/90 yd per 50 g/1³/₄ oz ball.

Rowan Felted Tweed: a lightweight merino wool, alpaca and viscose/rayon yarn; approximately 175 m/186 yd per 50 g/1³/₄ oz balls.

Rowan Magpie Tweed: a fisherman's medium-weight yarn (100% pure new wool); approximately 170 m/182 yd per 100 g/3¹/₂ oz hanks.

Rowan True 4 ply Botany: a 4 ply yarn (100% pure new wool); approximately 170 m/182 yd per 50 g/1³/₄ oz ball.

Rowan 4 ply Cotton: a 4 ply yarn (100% cotton); approximately 170 m/182 yd per 50 g/1³/₄ oz ball.

Rowan Wool Cotton: a double knitting yarn (50% merino, 50% cotton); approximately 113 m/122 yd per 50 g/1³/₄ oz ball.

Jaeger Aqua: a mercerized cotton yarn (100% cotton); approximately 106 m/115 yd per 50 g/1³/₄ oz ball.

Jaeger Cashmere 4 ply: a 4 ply yarn (90% cashmere, 10% polyamide); approximately 98 m/108 yd per 25 g/⁷/₈ oz ball.

Jaeger Baby Merino 4 ply: a 4 ply yarn (100% pure new wool); approximately 183 m/200 yd per 50 g/1³/₄ oz ball.

Jaeger Matchmaker Merino 4 ply: a 4 ply yarn (100% merino wool); approximately 183 m/200 yd per 50 g/1³/₄ oz ball.

Jaeger Persia: an 82% extra fine merino wool, 18% polyamide; approximately 100 m/109 yd per 50 g/1³/₄ oz ball

Jaeger Pure Cotton: a double knitting-weight cotton yarn (100% cotton); approximately 112 m/123 yd per 50 g/1³/₄ oz ball.

JACKET, TROUSERS, SHORTS AND SHOES

AN EASY-TO-KNIT OUTFIT THAT CAN BE EMBROIDERED TO CREATE A PERSONAL FINISH.

JACKET

BACK

With 3¼ mm (UK 10/US 3) needles, cast on 67 [73, 79] sts.

1st row (RS): K1, (p1, k1) to end.

This row forms moss st.

Rep this row 3 times more.

Change to 3¾ mm (UK 9/US 5) needles.

Next row (RS): Moss st 3, k to last 3 sts, moss st 3.

Next row: Moss st 3, p to last 3 sts, moss st 3.

Rep last 2 rows twice more.

Beg with a k row, now work in st st until back meas 13 [17, 19] cm (5 [6½, 7½] in) from cast-on edge, ending with a WS row.

Shape armholes

Cast off 3 sts at beg of next 2 rows. 61 [67, 73] sts.

Next row (RS): K2, sl 1, k1, psso, k to last 4 sts, k2tog, k2.

Next row: P2, p2tog, p to last 4 sts, p2tog tbl, p2.

Working all armhole decreases as set by last 2 rows, dec 1 st at each end of every row until 49 [53, 57] sts rem.

Cont straight until back meas 25 [28, 31] cm (9¾ [11, 12¼] in) from cast-on edge, ending with a WS row.

Shape shoulders

Cast off 14 [15, 16] sts at beg of next 2 rows.

Leave rem 21 [23, 25] sts on a holder for back neck.

LEFT FRONT

With 3¼ mm (UK 10/US 3) needles, cast on 31 [35, 39] sts.

Work 4 rows in moss st as for back.

Change to 3¾ mm (UK 9/US 5) needles.

Next row (RS): Moss st 3, k to end.

Next row: P to last 3 sts, moss st 3.

Rep last 2 rows twice more.

Beg with a k row, now work in st st until left front matches back to start of armhole shaping, ending with a WS row.

Shape armhole

Cast off 3 sts at beg of next row. 28 [32, 36] sts.

Work 1 row.

Working all armhole decreases as for back, dec 1 st at armhole edge

MATERIALS

Jacket

3 [4, 5] x 50 g balls of Rowan Cotton Glace in white

Pair each of 3¼ mm (UK 10/US 3) and 3¾ mm (UK 9/US 5) knitting needles

5 buttons

Trousers

3 [4, 4] x 50 g balls of Rowan Cotton Glace in white

Shorts

3 [3, 4] x 50 g balls of Rowan Cotton Glace in white

Trousers or Shorts

Pair each of 3¼ mm (UK 10/US 3) and 3¾ mm (UK 9/US 5) knitting needles

2 press fasteners

Shoes

1 x 50 g ball of Rowan Cotton Glace in white

Pair of 2¾ mm (UK 12/US 2) knitting needles

2 buttons

For optional embroidery

Small amounts of same yarn in pink, pale yellow, pale blue, lilac and pale lilac

MEASUREMENTS

	6	12	18 months
To fit age	6	12	18 months
Cardigan			
Actual measurement	58	63	69 cm
	23	25	27 in
Length	25	28	31 cm
	9¾	11	12¼ in
Sleeve seam	14	17	20 cm
	5½	6½	7¾ in
Trousers and Shorts			
Waist to crotch	21	24	28 cm
	8¼	9½	11 in
Trouser inside leg	15	19	23 cm
	6	7½	9 in
Shorts inside leg	7.5	9.5	11.5 cm
	3	3¾	4½ in
Shoes			
To fit age	3	6–12	12 months

ABBREVIATIONS

See page 20.

TENSION

23 sts and 32 rows to l0 cm (4 in) measured over st st using 3¾ mm (UK 9/US 5) needles.

of every row until 22 [25, 27] sts.
Cont straight until left front meas 20 [23, 26] cm (7¾ [9, 10¼] in) from cast-on edge, ending with a RS row.
Shape neck
Next row (WS): P5 [6, 7] and slip these sts onto a safety pin, p to end. 17 [19, 21] sts.
Dec 1 st at neck edge on every row until 14 [15, 16] sts rem.
Cont straight until left front matches back to start of shoulder shaping, ending with a WS row.
Shape shoulder
Cast off rem 14 [15, 16] sts.

RIGHT FRONT
Work as for left front, reversing all shapings.

SLEEVES
With 3¼ mm (UK 10/US 3) needles, cast on 27 [31, 35] sts.
Work 4 rows in moss st as for back.
Change to 3¾ mm (UK 9/US 5) needles.
Beg with a k row, now work in st st, inc 1 st at each end of next and every foll 3rd [4th, 5th] row to 53 [55, 59] sts.
Cont straight until sleeve meas 14 [17, 20] cm (5½ [6½, 7¾] in) from cast-on edge, ending with a WS row.
Shape top
Cast off 3 sts at beg of next 2 rows, then 2 sts at beg of foll 6 rows. 35 [37, 41] sts.
Dec 1 st each

end of next 8 rows. 19 [21, 25] sts.
Cast off 2 sts beg of next 2 rows, then 3 sts at beg of foll 2 rows.
Cast off rem 9 [11, 15] sts.

BUTTON BORDER
With 3¼ mm (UK 10/US 3) needles, cast on 5 sts.
Work in moss st as given for back until border, when slightly stretched, fits up left front opening edge from cast-on edge to neck shaping, ending with a WS row.
Break yarn and leave sts on a holder.
Sew border in place.
Mark positions for 5 buttons on this border – first one 1 cm (⅜ in) up from lower edge, last one 1 cm (⅜ in) down from neck edge and rem 3 evenly spaced between.

BUTTONHOLE BORDER
Work to match button border, making buttonholes to correspond with positions marked for buttons as follows:
Buttonhole row (RS): Moss st 2, yrn, p2tog, moss st 1.
When border is complete, do NOT break yarn.

COLLAR
Join shoulder seams.
With 3¼ mm (UK 10/US 3) needles and RS facing, cast off first 3 sts of buttonhole border (1 st on right needle after cast-off), work tog last st of border with first st on right front safety pin, k rem 4 [5, 6] sts from safety pin, pick up and k 12 sts up right side of neck, k 21 [23, 25] sts from back, pick up and k 12 sts down left side of neck, then k first 4 [5, 6] sts from left front safety pin, work tog last st from safety pin with first of button border, moss st rem 4 sts of border.
Keeping moss st correct as set by borders, proceed as follows:
Cast off 3 sts at beg of next row. 57 [61, 65] sts.
Work 7 rows in moss st.
Change to 3¾ mm (UK 9/US 5) needles and work a further 15 rows.
Cast off loosely in moss st.

TO MAKE UP
Join side seams, leaving seams open for first 10 rows.
Join sleeve seams. Insert sleeves. Sew on buttons.
Embroidery (optional)
Using contrasting colours, embroider flowers at random over fronts, back and sleeves. For each flower, embroider 5 lazy daisy stitches radiating out from one point (see pages 18 to 19 for stitch details).

TROUSERS AND SHORTS

LEGS (make 2)
With 3¼ mm (UK 10/US 3) needles, cast on 55 [65, 73] sts.
1st row (RS): K1, (p1, k1) to end.
This row forms moss st.
Rep this row 3 times more.
Next row (RS): Moss st 2 [4, 4], inc in next st, *moss st 6 [7, 8], inc in next st, rep from * to last 3 [4, 5] sts, moss st 3 [4, 5].
63 [73, 81] sts.
Change to 3¾ mm (UK 9/US 5) needles.
Beg with a k row, now work in st st until work meas 21 [24, 28] cm (8¼ [9½, 11] in) from cast-on edge, ending with a WS row.
Mark each end of last row.

TO MAKE UP

Join centre front and back seams from cast-on edge to markers. Join leg seams. Sew one end of each strap inside waist edge at back. Sew one half of press fastener to free end of strap and other section to waist edge at front to correspond.

Embroidery (optional)

Using contrasting colours, embroider flowers at random. For each flower, embroider 5 lazy daisy stitches radiating out from one point (see pages 18 to 19 for stitch details).

SHOES

RIGHT SHOE

With 2¾ mm (UK 12/US 2) needles, cast on 28 [32, 36] sts.

Knit 1 row.

1st row (RS): K1, yfwd, k12 [14, 16], yfwd, (k1, yfwd) twice, k12 [14, 16], yfwd, k1. 33 [37, 41] sts.

2nd, 4th, 6th, 8th and 10th rows: K to end, working (k1 tbl) into each (yfwd) of previous row.

3rd row: K2, yfwd, k12 [14, 16], yfwd, k2, yfwd, k3, yfwd, k12 [14, 16], yfwd, k2. 38 [42, 46] sts.

5th row: K3, yfwd, k12 [14, 16], yfwd, (k4, yfwd) twice, k12 [14, 16], yfwd, k3. 43 [47, 51] sts.

7th row: K4, yfwd, k12 [14, 16], yfwd, k5, yfwd, k6, yfwd, k12 [14, 16], yfwd, k4. 48 [52, 56] sts.

9th row: K5, yfwd, k12 [14, 16], yfwd, (k7, yfwd) twice, k12 [14, 16], yfwd, k5. 53 [57, 61] sts.

11th row: K9 [9, 8], yfwd, (k7 [8, 9], yfwd) 5 times, k9 [8, 8]. 59 [63, 67] sts.

12th row: As 2nd row.

Next row (RS): K1, (p1, k1) to end.

This row forms moss st.

Rep last row 11 times more.

Shape instep

1st row (RS): Moss st 23 [25, 27], k12, sl 1, k1, psso, turn.

2nd row: Sl 1, p11, p2tog, turn.

Trousers only

Cont in st st, dec 1 st at each end of next and every foll 6th [8th, 10th] row until 57 [67, 75] sts rem.

Cont without shaping until work meas 13.5 [17.5, 21.5] cm (5¼ [6¾, 8½] in) from markers, ending with a RS row.

Shorts only

Cont in st st, dec 1 st at each end of next and every foll 3rd [4th, 5th] row until 57 [67, 75] sts rem.

Cont without shaping until work meas 6 [8, 10] cm (2¼ [3, 4] in) from markers, ending with a RS row.

Trousers and Shorts

Next row (WS): P1, p2tog, *p4 [5, 6], p2tog, rep from * to last 0 [1, 0] st, p0 [1, 0].

47 [57, 65] sts.

Change to 3¼ mm (UK 10/US 3) needles and work in moss st for 4 rows.

Cast off in moss st.

STRAPS (make 2)

With 3¼ mm (UK 10/US 3) needles, cast on 13 sts.

1st row (RS): K2, (p1, k1) to last st, k1.

2nd row: K1, (p1, k1) to end.

Rep these 2 rows until strap meas 35 [40, 46] cm (13¾ [15¾, 18] in) from cast-on edge.

Cast off in rib.

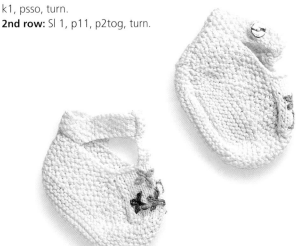

3rd row: Sl 1, k11, sl 1, k1, psso, turn.
Rep 2nd and 3rd rows 6 [7, 8] times more, and then
2nd row again.
Break yarn.
Rejoin yarn with RS facing and cast off, decreasing one st at each
corner as before and leaving 3 sts at centre of instep on a safety pin.
Join sole and back heel seam.

Shape heel strap
With RS facing, starting and ending 8 sts either side of heel seam,
pick up and k 17 sts along heel.
Work 1 row in moss st.**

Next row: Cast on 3 sts, moss st to end, turn and cast on 19 sts.
Work a further 2 rows in moss st.

Buttonhole row: Moss st 2, yrn, work 2 tog, moss st to end.
***Work 1 row in moss st.
Cast off.

Shape instep strap
With right side facing, rejoin yarn to 3 sts of instep left on
safety pin.
Work in moss st for 6 [7, 8] cm (2¼ [2¾, 3] in).
Cast off.
Fold last 2 cm (¾ in) to inside and stitch in place.
Thread heel strap through this loop. Sew on button to correspond
with buttonhole.

Embroidery (optional)
Using contrasting colours, embroider flowers onto instep. For each
flower, embroider 5 lazy daisy stitches radiating out from one point
(see pages 18 to 19 for stitch details).

LEFT SHOE
Work as given for right shoe to **.

Next row: Cast on 19 sts, moss st to end, turn and cast on 3 sts.
Work 2 rows in moss st.

Buttonhole row: Moss to last 4 sts, work 2 tog, yrn, moss st
2. Complete to match right shoe from ***.

A variation for everyday wear,
knitted in lilac.

27

SHORT BOLERO JACKET

THIS SMART JACKET WILL BECOME BABY'S SUNDAY BEST.

MATERIALS

3 x 50 g balls of Jaeger Aqua in pale green
Pair each of 3¼ mm (UK 10/US 3) and 3¾ mm (UK 9/US 5)
knitting needles
3 buttons

MEASUREMENTS

To fit age	3–6 months
Actual measurement	58 cm
	23 in
Length	22 cm
	8½ in
Sleeve seam	7 cm
	2¾ in

ABBREVIATIONS

See page 20.

TENSION

23 sts and 32 rows to 10 cm (4 in) measured over patt
using 3¾ mm (UK 9/US 5) needles.

LEFT FRONT

With 3¼ mm (UK 10/US 3) needles, cast on 23 sts.
1st row (RS): (K1, p1) to last 3 sts, k1, inc in next st, p1.
2nd row: Inc in first st, (k1, p1) to last st, k1.
Rep 1st and 2nd rows twice. 29 sts.
Change to 3¾ mm (UK 9/US 5) needles.
Next row (RS): K4, (k3, inc in next st) 5 times (k1, p1) twice, k1.
34 sts.
Next row: (K1, p1) twice, k1, p to end.
Now work in patt as follows:
1st row (RS): K3, (p1, k3) to last 7 sts, inc in next st, k1, (k1, p1)
twice, k1.
2nd row: (K1, p1) twice, k1, p to end.
3rd row: K1, (p1, k3) to last 10 sts, p1, k2, inc in next st, k1, (k1, p1)
twice, k1.
4th row: As 2nd row.
Last 4 rows form patt with front opening edge 5 sts still worked in
moss st. Keeping patt and moss st correct as now set, proceed as
follows:
5th row: Patt to last 7 sts, inc in next st, k1, moss st 5.
Work 1 row.
Rep last 2 rows once more. 38 sts.
(Front shaping is now complete.)
Cont in patt with moss st border until work meas 12 cm (4¾ in)
from cast-on edge, ending with a WS row.
Shape armhole and front slope
Keeping patt and border correct, proceed as follows:
Next row: Cast off 3 sts, patt to last 7 sts, k2tog, moss st 5. 34 sts.
Work 1 row.
**Dec 1 st at armhole edge on next and foll 2 alt rows *at the same
time* dec 1 st at front slope edge as set on every 3rd row from
previous dec. 29 sts.
Dec 1 st at front slope edge only on every foll 3rd row from previous
dec until 22 sts rem.
Cont straight until work meas 22 cm (8½ in) from cast-on edge,
ending at armhole edge.
Shape shoulder
Cast off 9 sts at beg of next row, then 8 sts at beg of foll alt row.
Work 18 rows in moss st on rem 5 sts.
Cast off.
Mark positions for 3 buttons along moss st border – first button
to be level with first row worked after front shaping is complete,
3rd button to be level with first front slope dec and rem button
midway between.

RIGHT FRONT

With 3¼ mm (UK 10/US 3) needles, cast on 23 sts.
1st row (RS): Inc in first st, (p1, k1) to end.

2nd row: (K1, p1) to last 2 sts, inc in next st, k1.

Rep 1st and 2nd rows twice. 29 sts.

Change to 3¾ mm (UK 9/US 5) needles.

Next row (RS): (K1, p1) twice, k1, (inc in next st, k3) 5 times, k4. 34 sts.

Next row: P to last 5 sts, (k1, p1) twice, k1.

Now work in patt as follows:

1st row (RS): (K1, p1) twice, k1, inc in next st, k1, (k3, p1) to last 3 sts, k3.

2nd row: P to last 5 sts, (k1, p1) twice, k1.

3rd row: (K1, p1) twice, k1, inc in next st, (k3, p1) to last st, k1.

4th row: As 2nd row.

Last 4 rows form patt with front opening edge 5 sts still worked in moss st.

Keeping patt and moss st correct as now set, proceed as follows:

5th row: Moss st 5, inc in next st, patt to end.

Work 1 row.

Rep last 2 rows once more. 38 sts.

(Front shaping is now complete.)

Next row (RS) (buttonhole row): K1, p1, yrn, p2tog, k1, patt to end.

Working 2nd buttonhole in same way as first to correspond with position marked on left front, cont in patt with moss st border until work meas 12 cm (4¾ in) from cast-on edge, ending with a WS row.

Shape armhole and front slope

Keeping patt and border correct, proceed as follows:

Next row (RS) (buttonhole row): K1, p1, yrn, p2tog, k1, sl 1, k1, psso, patt to end.

Cast off 3 sts at beg of next row. 34 sts.

Complete as for left front from **, reversing all shapings.

BACK

With 3¼ mm (UK 10/US 3) needles, cast on 63 sts.

Work 6 rows in moss st as for left front, inc 4 sts evenly across last row. 67 sts.

Change to 3¾ mm (UK 9/US 5) needles.

Next row (RS): Knit.

Next row: Purl.

Now work in patt as follows:

1st row (RS): (K3, p1) to last 3 sts, k3.

2nd row: Purl.

3rd row: K1, p1, (k3, p1) to last st, k1.

4th row: As 2nd row.

Last 4 rows form patt.

Cont in patt until back matches fronts to start of armhole shaping, ending with a WS row.

Shape armholes

Keeping patt correct, cast off 3 sts at beg of next 2 rows. 61 sts.

Dec 1 st at both ends of next and foll 2 alt rows. 55 sts.

Cont straight until back matches fronts to start of shoulder shaping,

ending with a WS row.

Shape shoulders

Cast off 9 sts at beg of next 2 rows, then 8 sts at beg of foll 2 rows.

Cast off rem 21 sts for back neck.

SLEEVES

With 3¼ mm (UK 10/US 3) needles, cast on 35 sts.

Work 5 rows in moss st as for back.

Next row (WS): Moss st 3, (inc in next st, moss st 3) 8 times. 43 sts.

Change to 3¾ mm (UK 9/US 5) needles.

Next row: Knit.

Next row: Purl.

Now work in patt as for back until sleeve meas 7 cm (2¾ in) from cast-on edge, ending with a WS row.

Shape top

Keeping patt correct, cast off 3 sts at beg of next 2 rows. 37 sts.

Dec 1 st at both ends of next and every foll alt row until 17 sts rem, then on every row until 11 sts rem.

Cast off.

TO MAKE UP

Join shoulder seams. Join ends of bands at back neck and stitch neatly into position across back of neck. Join side seams. Join sleeve seams. Insert sleeves.

Sew on buttons.

THREE-IN-ONE GUERNSEYS

THREE TWISTS ON A CLASSIC THEME MAKE THREE STYLES TO CHOOSE FROM: A SIMPLE STOCKING STITCH VERSION, A SWEATER AND A TUNIC, BOTH IN MOSS AND GARTER STITCH.

STOCKING STITCH GUERNSEY

BACK

With 3¼ mm (UK 10/US 3) needles, cast on 58 [62, 66, 70] sts.
Beg with a k row, work 6 rows in st st.
1st row (RS): K2, (p2, k2) to end.
2nd row: P2, (k2, p2) to end.
Rep last 2 rows twice more.
Change to 4 mm (UK 8/US 6) needles.**
Beg with a k row, now work in st st until back meas 28 [32, 36, 40] cm
(11 [12½, 14, 15¾] in) from lower edge *allowing first 6 rows to roll to RS*, ending with a WS row.
Shape shoulders
Cast off 18 [19, 19, 20] sts at beg of next 2 rows.
Leave rem 22 [24, 28, 30] sts on a holder.

FRONT

Work as for back until 16 [16, 20, 20] rows less have been worked than on back to start of shoulder shaping, ending with a WS row.

MATERIALS

4 [5, 6, 7] x 50 g balls of Rowan Handknit DK Cotton in taupe, pale blue or ecru
Pair each of 3¼ mm (UK 10/US 3) and 4 mm (UK 8/US 6) knitting needles

MEASUREMENTS

To fit age	6	9	12	18 months
To fit chest size	46	51	56	61 cm
	18	20	22	24 in
Actual measurement	58	62	66	70 cm
	22¾	24½	26	27½ in
Length	28	32	36	40 cm
	11	12½	14	15¾ in
Sleeve seam	18	22	26	29 cm
	7	8½	10¼	11½ in

ABBREVIATIONS
See page 20.

TENSION
20 sts and 28 rows to l0 cm (4 in) measured over st st using 4 mm (UK 8/US 6) needles.

Shape neck

Next row (RS): K24 [25, 26, 27], turn and work this side first.

Dec 1 st at neck edge on next 6 [6, 7, 7] rows. 18 [19, 19, 20] sts.

Work 3 [3, 6, 6] rows, ending with a WS row.

Cast off.

With RS facing, slip centre 10 [12, 14, 16] sts onto a holder, rejoin yarn to rem sts, k to end.

Dec 1 st at neck edge on next 6 [6, 7, 7] rows. 18 [19, 19, 20] sts.

Work 10 [10, 13, 13] rows, ending with a WS row.

Cast off.

SLEEVES

With 3¼ mm (UK 10/US 3) needles, cast on 34 [38, 38, 42] sts.

Beg with a k row, work 6 rows in st st.

Now work 5 rows in rib as for back.

Next row (WS): Rib 3 [5, 3, 3], inc in next st, *rib 8 [8, 5, 6], inc in next st, rep from * to last 3 [5, 4, 3] sts, rib 3 [5, 4, 3]. 38 [42, 44, 48] sts.

Change to 4 mm (UK 8/US 6) needles.

Beg with a k row, now work in st st, inc 1 st at each end of 5th and every foll 5th [6th, 7th, 8th] row until there are 50 [54, 58, 62] sts.**

Cont straight until sleeve meas 18 [22, 26, 29] cm

(7 [8½, 10¼, 11½] in) from lower edge *allowing first 6 rows to roll to RS*, ending with a WS row.
Cast off loosely.

NECK BORDER

Join right shoulder seam.
With RS facing and 3¼ mm (UK 10/US 3) needles, pick up and k 9 [9, 12, 12] sts down left side of neck, k 10 [12, 14, 16] sts from front, pick up and k 13 [13, 16, 16] sts up right side of neck, then k 22 [24, 28, 30] sts from back.
54 [58, 70, 74] sts.
Knit 1 row, then purl 2 rows.
Beg with 1st row, work 4 rows in rib as for back.
Beg with a k row, work 4 rows in st st.
Cast off loosely.

BUTTON BORDER

With RS facing and 3¼ mm (UK 10/US 3) needles, starting at top of neck border rib, pick up and k 22 [22, 26, 26] sts along left shoulder edge of neck border and back.
Beg with a 2nd row, work 5 rows in rib as for back.
Cast off in rib.

BUTTONHOLE BORDER

With RS facing and 3¼ mm (UK 10/US 3) needles, pick up and k 22 [22, 26, 26] sts along left shoulder edge of back and neck border, ending at top of neck border rib.
Beg with a 2nd row, work 1 row in rib as for back.
Next row (RS): Rib 2, (cast off 2 sts, rib until there are 6 [6, 8, 8] sts on right needle after cast-off) twice, cast off 2 sts, rib to end.

Next row: Rib to end, casting on 2 sts over those cast off on previous row.
Work a further 2 rows in rib.
Cast off in rib.

TO MAKE UP

Lay buttonhole border over button border and sew together at armhole edge. Fold sleeves in half lengthways, then placing folds to shoulder seams, sew sleeves in position. Join side and sleeve seams, reversing seam for st st roll at lower edges.

MOSS AND GARTER STITCH GUERNSEY

BACK

Work as for back of Stocking Stitch Guernsey to **.
Beg with a k row, now work in st st until back meas 15 [16, 19, 21] cm (6 [6¼, 7½, 8¼] in) from lower edge *allowing first 6 rows to roll to RS*, ending with a WS row.
Now work in yoke patt as follows:
1st and 2nd rows: Knit.
3rd and 4th rows: Purl.
5th row: Knit.
6th row: (K1, p1) to end.
7th row: (P1, k1) to end.
8th to 11th rows: As 6th and 7th rows twice.
12th row: As 6th row.
These 12 rows form patt.
Cont in patt until back meas 28 [32, 36, 40] cm (11 [12½, 14, 15¾] in) from lower edge *allowing first 6 rows to roll to RS*, ending with a WS row.

Beg with a p row, now work in st st until back meas 10 [11, 14, 17] cm (4 [4¼, 5½, 6½] in) from cast-on edge, ending with a WS row.
Now work in yoke patt as follows:
1st and 2nd rows: Knit.
3rd and 4th rows: Purl.
5th row: Knit.
6th row: (K1, p1) to end.
7th row: (P1, k1) to end.
8th to 11th rows: As 6th and 7th rows twice.
12th row: As 6th row.
These 12 rows form patt.
Cont in patt until back meas 28 [32, 36, 40] cm (11 [12½, 14, 15¾] in) from cast-on edge, ending with a WS row.

Shape shoulders
Cast off 18 [19, 19, 20] sts at beg of next 2 rows.
Leave rem 22 [24, 28, 30] sts on a holder.

FRONT
Work as for back until 16 [16, 20, 20] rows less have been worked than on back to start of shoulder shaping, ending with a WS row.
Keeping patt correct, complete as for front of Stocking Stitch Guernsey from start of neck shaping.

SLEEVES
With 3¼ mm (UK 10/US 3) needles, cast on 34 [38, 38, 42] sts.
Work 4 rows in moss st as for back.
Next row (RS): Moss st 3 [5, 3, 3], inc in next st, *moss st 8 [8, 5, 6], inc in next st, rep from * to last 3 [5, 4, 3] sts, moss st 3 [5, 4, 3].
38 [42, 44, 48] sts.
Change to 4 mm (UK 8/US 6) needles.
Beg with a p row, now work in st st, inc 1 st at each end of 4th and every foll 4th [5th, 6th, 7th] row until there are 50 [54, 58, 62] sts.
Cont straight until sleeve meas 11 [15, 19, 22] cm (4¼ [6, 7½, 8½] in) from cast-on edge, ending with a WS row.
Now work 28 rows in patt as for back.
Cast off loosely.

NECK, BUTTON AND BUTTONHOLE BORDERS
Work as for neck, button and buttonhole borders of Stocking Stitch Guernsey.

TO MAKE UP
Work as for Stocking Stitch Guernsey, leaving side seams open for first 15 rows at lower edge.

Shape shoulders
Cast off 18 [19, 19, 20] sts at beg of next 2 rows.
Leave rem 22 [24, 28, 30] sts on a holder.

FRONT
Work as for back until 16 [16, 20, 20] rows less have been worked than on back to start of shoulder shaping, ending with a WS row.
Keeping patt correct, complete as for front of Stocking Stitch Guernsey from start of neck shaping.

SLEEVES
Work as for sleeves of Stocking Stitch Guernsey to **.
Cont straight until sleeve meas 14 [18, 22, 25] cm (5½ [7, 8½, 9¾] in) from lower edge *allowing first 6 rows to roll to RS*, ending with a WS row.
Now work 16 rows in patt as for back.
Cast off loosely.

NECK, BUTTON AND BUTTONHOLE BORDERS
Work as for neck, button and buttonhole borders of Stocking Stitch Guernsey.

TO MAKE UP
Work as for Stocking Stitch Guernsey.

MOSS AND GARTER STITCH TUNIC

BACK
With 3¼ mm (UK 10/US 3) needles, cast on 58 [62, 66, 70] sts.
1st row (RS): (K1, p1) to end.
2nd row: (P1, k1) to end.
These 2 rows form moss st.
Work a further 3 rows in moss st.
Change to 4 mm (UK 8/US 6) needles.
Next row (WS): Moss st 3, p to last 3 sts, moss st 3.
Next row: Moss st 3, k to last 3 sts, moss st 3.
Rep last 2 rows 4 times more.

HOUSE, HEART AND FLOWER JACKET AND HAT

YOUR BABY WILL STAND OUT FROM THE CROWD WITH THIS BRIGHT HOUSE, HEART AND FLOWER BANDED JACKET AND MATCHING HAT.

MATERIALS

4 x 50 g balls of Rowan Handknit DK Cotton in A (dark blue)
1 x 50 g ball of same yarn in each of B (mid-blue), C (lilac), D (green), E (yellow) and F (red)
Pair each of 3¼ mm (UK 10/US 3) and 4 mm (UK 8/US 6) knitting needles
4 buttons for Jacket

MEASUREMENTS

To fit age	6–12 months
Actual measurement	62 cm
	24½ in
Length	27 cm
	10½ in
Sleeve seam	20 cm
	7¾ in

ABBREVIATIONS
See page 20.

TENSION
20 sts and 28 rows to l0 cm (4 in) measured over st st using 4 mm (UK 8/US 6) needles.

NOTE
When working patt from charts, read charts from right to left on RS k rows and from left to right on WS p rows. Use separate lengths of yarn for each motif, twisting yarns together where they meet to avoid holes forming. For broken vertical lines, strand yarn not in use loosely across WS of work to keep fabric elastic.

JACKET

BACK AND FRONTS (Worked in one piece to armholes)
With 3¼ mm (UK 10/US 3) needles and A, cast on 122 sts.
Join in B.
1st row (RS): Using A p2, (using B k2, using A p2) to end.
2nd row: Using A k2, (using B p2, using A k2) to end.
Rep last 2 rows once more, inc 1 st at centre of last row. 123 sts.
Change to 4 mm (UK 8/US 6) needles.
Beg with a k row, now work in st st following back and fronts chart on page 39 as follows:

Cont straight until chart row 36 has been worked, thus ending with a WS row.
Divide for armholes
Next row (RS): Patt 30 sts and turn, leaving rem sts on a holder.
Work on this set of sts only for right front.
Work 9 rows, thus ending with chart row 46.
Shape front slope
Keeping patt correct, dec 1 st at beg of next and every foll alt row until 17 sts rem.
Work 2 rows, thus ending with chart row 73.
Shape shoulder
Cast off 9 at beg of next row.
Work 1 row.
Cast off rem 8 sts.
Shape back
With right side facing, rejoin yarn to rem sts and proceed as follows:
Next row (RS): Cast off 1 st, patt until there are 61 sts on right needle and turn, leaving rem sts on a holder.
Work on this set of sts only for back.
Cont straight until chart row 72 has been worked, ending with a WS row.
Shape shoulders
Cast off 9 sts at beg of next 2 rows and 8 sts at beg of foll 2 rows.
Leave rem 27 sts on a holder for back neck.
Shape left front
With right side facing, rejoin yarn to rem sts and proceed as follows:
Next row (RS): Cast off 1 st, patt to end. 30 sts.
Work 9 rows, thus ending with chart row 46.
Shape front slope
Keeping patt correct, dec 1 st at end of next and every foll alt row until 17 sts rem.
Work 1 row, thus ending with chart row 72.
Shape shoulder
Cast off 9 at beg of next row.
Work 1 row.
Cast off rem 8 sts.

SLEEVES
With 3¼ mm (UK 10/US 3) needles and A, cast on 34 sts.
Join in B.
Work 4 rows in 2 colour rib as for back and fronts, inc 3 sts evenly across last row. 37 sts.
Change to 4 mm (UK 8/US 6) needles.
Beg with a k row, now work in st st following sleeve and hat chart on page 38, inc 1 st at each end of 3rd and every foll 4th row until there are 55 sts, working inc sts into patt.
Cont straight until chart row 52 has been worked.
Cast off.

FRONT BORDER

Join shoulder seams.

With 3¼ mm (UK 10/US 3) needles and A, starting at right front cast-on edge, pick up and k 42 sts up right front opening edge to start of front slope shaping, 38 sts up right front slope to shoulder, k 27 sts from back dec 3 sts evenly, pick up and k 38 sts down left front slope to start of front slope shaping, then 42 sts down left front opening edge to cast-on edge. 184 sts.

Beg with a 2nd row, work 1 row in 2 colour rib as for back and fronts.

2nd row (RS) (buttonhole row): Rib 3, (yfwd, k2tog, rib 10) 3 times, yfwd, k2tog, rib to end.

Work a further 2 rows in rib.

Using A, cast off knitwise (on WS).

TO MAKE UP

Join sleeve seams. Sew sleeves into armholes, matching centre of cast-off edge to shoulder seam and sleeve seam to underarm. Sew on buttons.

HAT

With 3¼ mm (UK 10/US 3) needles and A, cast on 38 sts.

Work 4 rows in 2 colour rib as for back and fronts of jacket, dec 1 st at centre of last row. 37 sts.

Change to 4 mm (UK 8/US 6) needles.

Beg with a k row, now work in st st following sleeve and hat chart

below until chart row 36 has been worked. Cast off. Make another piece in same way.

TO MAKE UP

Join top and side seams.

Using A, make 2 twisted cords about 5 cm (2 in) long and 2 tassels. Attach a tassel to one end of each cord and other end of cord to corner of hat.

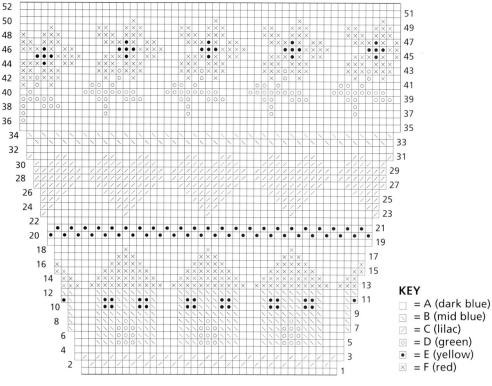

SLEEVE AND HAT CHART

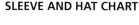

KEY
☐ = A (dark blue)
◩ = B (mid blue)
◪ = C (lilac)
◉ = D (green)
● = E (yellow)
✕ = F (red)

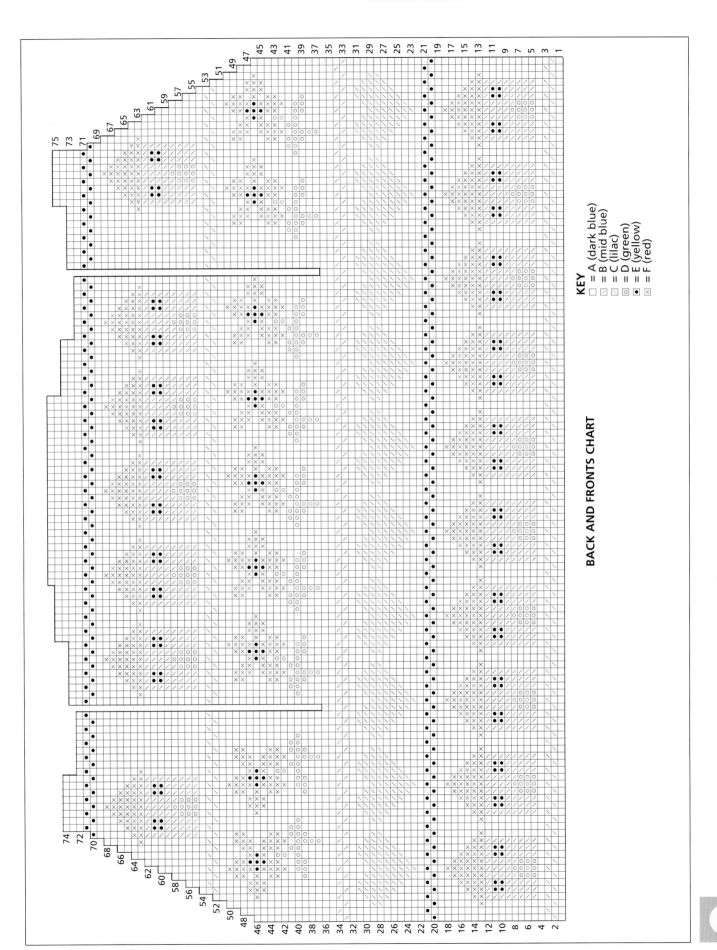

BACK AND FRONTS CHART

KEY

$\square$ = A (dark blue)
$\diagdown$ = B (mid blue)
$\diagdown$ = C (lilac)
$\boxdot$ = D (green)
$\bullet$ = E (yellow)
$\times$ = F (red)

GARTER STITCH STRIPED JUMPER, HAT AND BOOTIES

THIS OUTFIT IS SO SIMPLE IT'S IDEAL FOR BEGINNERS, QUICK TO KNIT, YET EFFECTIVE.

JUMPER

BACK

With 3¼ mm (UK 10/US 3) needles and A, cast on 64 [70, 76] sts.
Knit 3 rows.
1st to 4th rows: Using B knit.
5th to 8th rows: Using C knit.
9th to 12th rows: Using D knit.
13th to 16th rows: Using E knit.
17th to 20th rows: Using F knit.
21st to 24th rows: Using A knit.
These 24 rows form striped g st patt.
Cont in striped g st as set until back measures 22 [24, 26] cm
(8½ [9½, 10¼] in) from cast-on edge, ending with a WS row.
Shape neck
Next row (RS): K18 [20, 22], turn and work this side first.
Cont straight until back measures 24 [26, 28] cm (9½ [10¼, 11] in)
from cast-on edge, ending with a WS row.
Cast off.
With RS facing, slip centre 28 [30, 32] sts onto a st holder, rejoin
yarn to rem sts, k to end. Complete to match first side.

FRONT

Work as for back until front measures 21 [23, 25] cm (8¼ [9, 9¾] in)
from cast-on edge, ending with a WS row.
Shape neck
Next row (RS):
K18 [20, 22], turn and work this side first.
Cont straight until front measures 24 [26, 28] cm (9½ [10¼, 11] in)
from cast-on edge, ending with a WS row.
Cast off.

MATERIALS

2 [2, 3] x 50 g balls of Rowan Cotton Glace in A (lavender)
1 [1, 2] x 50 g balls of same yarn in each of B (pale green),
C (pink), D (white), E (blue) and F (yellow)
Pair each of 3 mm (UK 11/US 2/3) and 3¼ mm (UK 10/US 3)
knitting needles
3.5 mm (UK 9/US E4) crochet hook
2 buttons

MEASUREMENTS

Jumper

To fit age	3	6	9 months
Actual measurement	49	54	58 cm
	19½	21	23 in
Length	24	26	28 cm
	9½	10¼	11in
Sleeve seam	14	16	17.5cm
	5½	6¼	7 in

Hat and Booties
One size to fit age 3-9 months

ABBREVIATIONS

See page 20.

TENSION

26 sts and 50 rows to l0 cm (4 in) measured over g st using
3¼ mm (UK 10/US 3) knitting needles.

With RS facing, slip centre 28 [30, 32] sts onto a st holder, rejoin yarn to rem sts, k to end. Complete to match first side.

SLEEVES

With 3¼ mm (UK 10/US 3) needles and A, cast on 39 [44, 49] sts.
Starting with 3 rows using A, cont in striped g st as for back as follows:
Work 27 rows.
Change to 3 mm (UK 11/US 2/3) needles.
Starting with 3 rows using A (to reverse fabric for turn-back cuff), cont in striped g st as for back, inc 1 st at each end of 5th and every foll 7th [8th, 9th] row until there are 53 [58, 65] sts.
Cont straight until sleeve measures 19 [21, 23] cm (7½ [8¼, 9] in) from cast-on edge, ending with a WS row.
Cast off.

NECK BORDER

Join right shoulder seam.
With right side facing, using 3 mm (UK 11/US 2/3) needles and A, pick up and knit 11 sts down left side of front neck, k 28 [30, 32] sts from front, pick up and knit 11 sts up right side of front neck, and 7 sts down right side of back neck, k 28 [30, 32] sts from back, then pick up and knit 7 sts up left side of back neck. 92 [96, 100] sts.
Next row (WS): K5, sl 1, k1, psso, k2tog, k24 [26, 28], sl 1, k1, psso, k2tog, k14, sl 1, k1, psso, k2tog, k24 [26, 28], sl 1, k1, psso, k2tog, k9.
Cast off.

TO MAKE UP

Using A, make 2 buttonhole loops along front edge of left shoulder. Fold sleeves in half lengthways, then placing folds to shoulder seams, sew sleeves in position. Join side and sleeve seams, reversing sleeve seam for turn-back cuff. Sew on buttons.

HAT

EAR FLAPS (make 2)

Using 3¼ mm (UK 10/US 3) needles and B, cast on 6 sts.
Knit 1 row.
Starting with a further 2 rows in B (to complete this stripe), cont in striped g st as for jumper, inc 1 st at each end on next 4 rows, then on foll 3 alt rows. 20 sts.
Cont straight until 4 rows using A have been completed.
Break yarn and leave these sts on a st holder.

MAIN SECTION

Using 3¼ mm (UK 10/US 3) needles and B, cast on 14 sts, then, with RS facing, k across 20 sts of first ear flap, turn and cast on 32 sts, turn and k across 20 sts of second ear flap, turn and cast on 14 sts. 100 sts.
Cont in striped g st as set until main part measures 10 [12, 14] cm (4 [4¾, 5½] in) from cast-on edge, ending with a WS row.
Keeping striped g st correct, proceed as follows:
1st row (RS): K1, (k2tog, k7) to end. 89 sts.
Work 3 rows.

5th row: K1, (k2tog, k6) to end. 78 sts.
Work 1 row.
7th row: K1, (k2tog, k5) to end. 67 sts.
Work 1 row.
9th row: K1, (k2tog, k4) to end. 56 sts.
Work 1 row.
11th row: K1, (k2tog, k3) to end. 45 sts.
Work 1 row.
13th row: K1, (k2tog, k2) to end. 34 sts.
Work 1 row.
15th row: K1, (k2tog, k1) to end. 23 sts.
Work 1 row.
17th row: K1, (k2tog) to end. 12 sts.
Work 1 row.
Break off yarn and thread through rem sts. Pull up tight and fasten off securely. Join back seam.

Lower edging

With RS facing, using crochet hook and A, starting and ending at back seam, work one round of double crochet along entire lower edge of main section and ear flaps, ending with slip

stitch to first st, do NOT turn.
Now work one round of crab stitch (double crochet worked from left to right, instead of right to left) around lower edge, ending with slip stitch to first st.
Fasten off.

BOOTIES (make 2)

Using 3¼ mm (UK 10/US 3) needles and A, cast on 36 sts. Starting with 3 rows using A, cont in striped g st as for jumper as follows:

Work 27 rows, ending after 4 rows using A.
Shape instep
Next row (RS): K24, turn.
Next row: K12, turn.
Work a further 22 rows on these 12 sts only.
Break yarn.
With RS facing, rejoin yarn at end of last complete row worked, k first 12 sts before instep, pick up and knit 12 sts along first row end edge of instep, k 12 instep sts, then pick up and knit 12 sts along other row end edge of instep, k rem 12 sts. 60 sts.
Work a further 11 rows, thus ending with a WS row.
Break yarn.
Shape sole
Next row (RS): Slip first 24 sts onto right needle, rejoin yarn, k12 and turn.
Next row: K11, k2tog, turn.
Rep last row until 12 sts rem.
Next row: (K2tog) to end.
Rep last row once more.
Cast off rem 3 sts.
Join back seam.

Variation knitted in bright colours for a stronger look.

EMBROIDERED MOSS STITCH JACKET AND BOOTIES

WHAT COULD BE PRETTIER THAN AN EMBROIDERED MOSS STITCH JACKET FOR THE YOUNG BABY?

JACKET

BACK

With 3¼ mm (UK 10/US 3) needles, cast on 117 sts.
1st row (RS): K1, (p1, k1) to end.
This row forms moss st.
Cont in moss st until back meas 18 cm (7 in) from cast-on edge, ending with a WS row.
Next row (RS): (K1, p1, k1, p3tog) to last 3 sts, k1, p1, k1. 79 sts.
Cont in moss st until back meas 22 cm (8½ in) from cast-on edge, ending with a WS row.
Shape armholes
Cast off 3 sts at beg of next 2 rows. 73 sts.
Dec 1 st at each end of next 6 rows. 61 sts.
Cont straight until back meas 32 cm (12½ in) from cast-on edge, ending with a WS row.
Shape shoulders
Cast off 10 sts at beg of next 4 rows.
Cast off rem 21 sts.

MATERIALS

4 x 50 g balls of Rowan True 4 ply Botany in cream
Small amounts of same yarn in each of dark pink, pink, light pink, green and blue for embroidery
5 buttons
Pair of 3¼ mm (UK 10/US 3) knitting needles for jacket
Pair of 2¾ mm (UK 12/US 2) knitting needles for booties

MEASUREMENTS

To fit age	3–9 months
Actual measurement	56 cm
	22¼ in
Length	32 cm
	12½ in
Sleeve seam	17 cm
	6½ in

ABBREVIATIONS
See page 20.

TENSION
28 sts and 40 rows to 10 cm (4 in) measured over moss st using 3¼ mm (UK 10/US 3) needles.

LEFT FRONT

With 3¼ mm (UK 10/US 3) needles, cast on 65 sts.
Work in moss st as for back for 18 cm (7 in), ending with a WS row.
Next row (RS): (K1, p1, k1, p3tog) to the last 5 sts, (k1, p1) twice, k1. 45 sts.
Cont in moss st until left front matches back to start of armhole shaping, ending with a WS row.
Shape armhole
Cast off 3 sts at beg of next row. 42 sts.
Work 1 row.
Dec 1 st at armhole edge of next 6 rows. 36 sts.
Cont straight until left front meas 28 cm (11 in) from cast-on edge, ending with a RS row.
Shape neck
Cast off 7 sts at beg of next row. 29 sts.
Dec 1 st at neck edge on every row until 20 sts rem.
Cont straight until left front matches back to start of shoulder shaping, ending with a WS row.
Shape shoulder
Cast off 10 sts at beg of next row.
Work 1 row.
Cast off rem 10 sts.

RIGHT FRONT

With 3¼ mm (UK 10/US 3) needles, cast on 65 sts.
Work in moss st as for back for 17 cm (6½ in), ending with a WS row.
Next row (RS) (buttonhole row): Moss st 3, cast off 3 sts, moss st to end.
Next row: Moss st to end, casting on 3 sts over those cast off on previous row.
Complete to match left front, reversing all shapings and making 4 more buttonholes each 2.5 cm (1 in) apart.

SLEEVES

With 3¼ mm (UK 10/US 3) needles, cast on 43 sts.
Work 6 rows in moss st as for back.
Beg with a k row, work 12 rows in st st.
Now cont in moss st, inc 1 st at each end of next and every foll 4th row until there are 67 sts.
Cont straight until sleeve meas 17 cm (6½ in) from cast-on edge, ending with a WS row.
Shape top
Cast off 3 sts at beg of next 2 rows. 61 sts.
Dec 1 st at each end of every row until 25 sts rem.
Cast off.

COLLAR

With 3¼ mm (UK 10/US 3) needles, cast on 71 sts.
Work in moss st as for back for 6 rows.
7th row (RS): Moss st 6, k59, moss st 6.
8th row: Moss st 6, p59, moss st 6.
Rep 7th and 8th rows 7 times more and then 7th row again.
Work 5 rows in moss st.
Cast off 10 sts at beg of next 4 rows.
Cast off rem 31 sts.

TO MAKE UP

Sew shoulder seams. Sew shaped cast-off edge of collar to neck edge, positioning ends of collar 3 sts in from front opening edges. Join side seams. Join sleeve seams. Insert sleeves. Sew on buttons.

Embroidery

Embroider flowers, leaves and stems onto ends of collar and around cuffs as follows: With dark pink, pink and light pink, embroider flowers by working 5 lazy daisy stitches radiating out from one point. With blue, embroider a French knot at centre of each flower. With green, embroider stems using stem stitch, and add in leaves made by working one individual lazy daisy stitch near stem (see pages 18 to 19 for stitch details).

BOOTIES (make 2)

With 2¾ mm (UK 12/US 2) needles, cast on 39 sts.
1st row (RS): K1, (p1, k1) to end.
This row forms moss st.
Work in moss st for a further 5 rows.
Beg with a k row, work 20 rows in st st.
Change to 3¼ mm (UK 10/US 3) needles.
Shape ankle
1st row (RS): K7, k2tog, (k8, k2tog) to end. 35 sts.
2nd row: K1, (p1, k1) to end.
3rd row: P1, (k1, p1) to end.
4th row: (K1, p2tog, yrn, p1) to last 3 sts, k1, p1, k1.
5th row: As 3rd row.
6th row: As 2nd row.
Shape instep
Next row (RS): K23, turn.
Next row: P11, turn.
Beg next row with k1, work 24 rows in moss st on these 11 sts.
Break yarn.
With RS facing, rejoin yarn at end of first set of 12 sts, pick up and
k 15 sts along first side of instep, moss st 11 instep sts, then pick up
and k 15 sts along other side of instep, then k rem 12 sts. 65 sts.
Beg next row with p1, work in moss st for 9 rows.
Shape sole
1st row (RS): K2tog, moss st 29, k3tog, moss st 29, k2tog.
Work 1 row.
3rd row: P2tog, moss st 27, p3tog, moss st 27, p2tog.
Work 1 row.
5th row: K2tog, moss st 25, k3tog, moss st 25, k2tog.
Work 1 row.
Cast off.

TO MAKE UP
Embroider flowers round ankle to
match embroidery on jacket (see
pages 18 to 19 for stitch details).
Join underfoot and back seam.
Make 2 twisted cords and 4 small
pompoms. Thread cords through
eyelet holes around ankle and sew
on pompoms to ends of cords.

*Jacket knitted in navy
to give a smart look.
Embroidered with
flowers in the same
colours used for the
cream jacket.*

BODYWARMER

THIS CUTE ZIPPED BODYWARMER HAS A COSY HOOD AND EARS.

BACK

With 4 mm (UK 8/US 6) needles cast on 42 [46, 50] sts.
Rib row 1 (RS): K2, (p2, k2) to end.
Rib row 2: P2, (k2, p2) to end.
Rep last 2 rows twice more, inc 1 st at each end of last row.
44 [48, 52] sts.
Change to 4½ mm (UK 7/US 7) needles and beg with a k row, cont in st st until back measures 12 [14.5, 17] cm (4¾ [5¾, 6½] in) from cast-on edge, ending with a WS row.

Shape armholes

Cast off 2 [3, 4] sts at beg of next 2 rows. 40 [42, 44] sts.
Dec 1 st at each end of next and foll 2 alt rows. 34 [36, 38] sts.
Work straight until back meas 24 [29, 34] cm (9½ [11½, 13¼ in) from cast-on edge, ending with a WS row.

Shape shoulders

Cast off 5 sts at beg of next 4 rows.
Leave rem 14 [16, 18] sts on a holder.

LEFT POCKET LINING

Using 4½ mm (UK 7/US 7) needles cast on 17 [18, 19] sts.
Beg with a k row, work 31 [35, 39] rows in st st.
Leave sts on a holder.

RIGHT POCKET LINING

Using 4½ mm (UK 7/US 7) needles cast on 17 [18, 19] sts.
Beg with a k row, work 32 [36, 40] rows in st st.
Leave sts on a holder.

LEFT FRONT

With 4 mm (UK 8/US 6) needles cast on 21 [21, 25] sts.
Rib row 1: (K2, p2) to last 5 sts, k5.
Rib row 2: K3, p2, (k2, p2) to end.
Rep the last 2 rows twice more, inc 2 [4, 2] sts evenly across last row. 23 [25, 27] sts.
Change to 4½ mm (UK 7/US 7) needles.
Next row (RS): Knit.
Next row: K3, p to end.
These 2 rows form patt.
Work in patt for a further 2 [4, 6] rows.

Shape pocket

Keeping patt correct, cast off 4 sts at beg of next row.
Work 1 row.
Dec 1 st at beg of next and every foll alt row until 6 [7, 8] sts rem, ending with a RS row.
Next row (WS): K3, p3 [4, 5], then p across sts of pocket lining. 23 [25, 27] sts.

MATERIALS

3 [4, 5] x 50 g balls of Jaeger Persia in grey
Pair each of 4 mm (UK 8/US 6) and 4½ mm (UK 7/US 7) knitting needles
20 [25, 30] cm (8 [10, 12] in) open ended zip fastener

MEASUREMENTS

To fit age	3	6–12	12–24 months
Actual measurement	55	60	65 cm
	21½	23½	25½ in
Length to shoulder	24	29	34 cm
	9½	11½	13¼ in

ABBREVIATIONS

See page 20.

TENSION

16 sts and 26 rows to l0 cm (4 in) measured over st st using 4½ mm (UK 7/US 7) needles.

Cont straight until left front matches back to start of armhole shaping, ending with a WS row.

Shape armhole

Keeping patt correct, cast off 2 [3, 4] sts at beg of next row. 21 [22, 23] sts.

Work 1 row.

Dec 1 st at armhole edge of next and foll alt row. 19 [20, 21] sts. Cont straight until left front meas 21 [26, 31] cm (8¼ [10¼, 12¼] in), ending with a RS row.

Shape neck

Cast off 4 [5, 6] sts at beg of next row. 15 sts.

Dec 1 st at neck edge of every row until 10 sts rem.

Work a few rows straight until left front matches back to shoulder, ending at armhole edge.

Shape shoulder

Cast off 5 sts at beg of next row.

Work 1 row.

Cast off rem 5 sts.

RIGHT FRONT

With 4 mm (UK 8/US 6) needles cast on 21 [21, 25] sts.

Rib row 1 (RS): K5, (p2, k2) to end.

Rib row 2: (P2, k2) to last 5 sts, p2, k3.

Rep last 2 rows twice more, inc 2 [4, 2] sts evenly across last row. 23 [25, 27] sts.

Change to 4½ mm (UK 7/US 7) needles.

Next row (RS): Knit.

Next row: P to last 3 sts, k3.

These 2 rows form patt.
Work in patt for a further 3 [5, 7] rows.

Shape pocket

Keeping patt correct, cast off 4 sts at beg of next row.
Work 1 row.
Dec 1 st at beg of next and every foll alt row until 6 [7, 8] sts rem, ending with a WS row.
Next row (RS): K6 [7, 8], then k across sts of pocket lining. 23 [25, 27] sts.
Cont straight until right front matches back to start of armhole shaping, ending with a RS row.

Shape armhole

Keeping patt correct, cast off 2 [3, 4] sts at beg of next row. 21 [22, 23] sts.
Dec 1 st at armhole edge of next and foll alt row. 19 [20, 21] sts.
Cont straight until right front meas 21 [26, 31] cm (8¼ [10¼, 12¼] in), ending with a WS row.

Shape neck

Cast off 4 [5, 6] sts at beg of next row. 15 sts.
Dec 1 st at neck edge of every row until 10 sts rem.
Work a few rows straight until right front matches back to shoulder, ending at armhole edge.

Shape shoulder

Cast off 5 sts at beg of next row.
Work 1 row.
Cast off rem 5 sts.

HOOD

With 4 mm (UK 8/US 6) needles cast on 16 sts, then with RS facing knit across 14 [16, 18] sts from back neck holder, then cast on a further 16 sts. 46 [48, 50] sts.
Next row (WS): P4 [3, 2], (inc purlwise in next st, p2) to end. 60 [63, 66] sts.
Beg with a k row, cont in st st until hood meas 17 [18, 19] cm (6½ [7, 7½] in), ending with a WS row.

Shape top

Next row (RS): Cast off 20 [21, 22] sts, k until there are 20 [21, 22] sts on right needle after cast-off, cast off rem 20 [21, 22] sts.
With WS facing, rejoin yarn to rem sts and p to end.
Cont in st st for a further 12 [12, 13] cm (4¾ [4¾, 5] in), ending with a WS row.
Leave sts on a holder.

HOOD BORDER

Join hood seams.
With RS facing and using 4 mm (UK 8/US 6) needles, pick up and k 27 [29, 30] sts evenly along right side of hood, k across 20 [21, 22] sts from holder, pick up and k 27 [28, 30] sts evenly along left side of hood. 74 [78, 82] sts.
Beg with rib row 2, work 3 rows in rib as for back.
Cast off in rib.

EARS (make 2)

Using 4½ mm (UK 7/US 7) needles cast on 12 sts.
Beg with a k row, work 6 rows in st st.
Dec 1 st at each end of next and foll alt row. 8 sts.
Purl 1 row.
Cast off.

EAR LININGS (make 2)

Work as for ears but using 4 mm (UK 8/US 6) needles.

POCKET EDGINGS

With right side facing and using 4 mm (UK 8/US 6) needles, pick up and k 26 sts evenly along pocket edge.
Beg with rib row 1, work 3 rows in rib as for back.
Cast off in rib.

ARMHOLE BORDERS

Join shoulder seams.
With right side facing and using 4 mm (UK 8/US 6) needles, pick up and k 58 [66, 74] sts evenly around armhole edge.
Beg with rib row 1, work 3 rows in rib as for back.
Cast off in rib.

TO MAKE UP

Sew cast-on edge of hood to front neck edges. With right sides together and leaving cast-on edges open, join ears and ear linings. Turn to right side and close opening. Sew in place. Sew pocket linings in place on inside. Join side and armhole border seams. Sew in zip.

JACKET WITH LACE EDGING

THE LACE EDGING GIVES THIS MATINEE JACKET A BEAUTIFUL
FINISHING TOUCH.

213 sts.

217

RIGHT FRONT

With 3¾ mm (UK 9/US 5) needles, cast on 54 sts.

1st row: (K1, p1) twice, k to end.

2nd row: P to last 4 sts, (p1, k1) twice.

These 2 rows set st st with front opening edge 4 sts worked in moss st.

Cont in st st with moss st border until right front meas 17 cm (6½ in) from cast-on edge, ending with a RS row.

Next row (WS): P2, p2tog, *p3tog, (p2tog) twice, p2, (p2tog) twice, rep from * to last 11 sts, p3tog, p2tog, p2, moss st 4. 32 sts.

Change to 3¼ mm (UK 10/US 3) needles and work 2 rows in moss st (as set by moss st border) across all sts.

Buttonhole row (RS): Moss st 2, yrn, p2tog, moss st to end.

Work 3 more rows in moss st.

Change to 3¾ mm (UK 9/US 5) needles and work in st st with moss st border as before for 3 rows, ending with a RS row.

Shape armhole

Keeping st st and moss st border correct, cast off 3 sts at beg of next row. 29 sts.

Dec 1 st at armhole edge of next row.

Work 1 row.

Buttonhole row (RS): Moss st 2, yrn, p2tog, k to last 2 sts, k2tog.

Work 1 row.

Dec 1 st at armhole edge of next row. 26 sts.

Work 15 rows, making 3rd buttonhole as before on 8th of these rows and ending with a WS row.

Shape neck

Next row (RS): Patt 7 sts and slip these 7 sts onto a safety pin, k to end. 19 sts.

**Dec 1 st at neck edge on every row until 14 sts rem.

Cont straight until armhole meas 10 cm (4 in), ending at armhole edge.

Shape shoulder

Cast off 7 sts at beg of next row.

Work 1 row.

Cast off rem 7 sts.

LEFT FRONT

With 3¾ mm (UK 9/US 5) needles, cast on 54 sts.

1st row: K to last 4 sts, (k1, p1) twice.

2nd row: (P1, k1) twice, p to end.

These 2 rows set st st with front opening edge 4 sts worked in moss st.

Cont in st st with moss st border until left front meas 17 cm (6½ in) from cast-on edge, ending with a RS row.

Next row (WS): Moss st 4, p2, p2tog, *p3tog, (p2tog) twice, p2, (p2tog) twice, rep from * to last 7 sts, p3tog, p2tog, p2. 32 sts.

Change to 3¼ mm (UK 10/US 3) needles and work 6 rows in

MATERIALS

4 x 50 g balls of Rowan Wool Cotton in red
Pair each of 3¼ mm (UK 10/US 3) and 3¾ mm (UK 9/US 5) knitting needles
4 buttons

MEASUREMENTS

To fit age	6–12 months
Actual measurement	51 cm
	20 in
Length	32 cm
	12½ in
Sleeve seam	16 cm
	6¼ in

ABBREVIATIONS

See page 20.

TENSION

22 sts and 30 rows to 10 cm (4 in) measured over st st using 3¾ mm (UK 9/US 5) needles.

moss st (as set by moss st border) across all sts.
Change to 3¾ mm (UK 9/US 5) needles and work in st st with
moss st border as before for 2 rows, ending with a WS row.

Shape armhole
Keeping st st and moss st border correct, cast off 3 sts at beg of
next row. 29 sts.
Work 1 row.
Dec 1 st at armhole edge of next and foll 2 alt rows. 26 sts.
Work 14 rows, ending with a RS row.

Shape neck
Next row (WS): Patt 7 sts and slip these 7 sts onto a safety pin,
k to end. 19 sts.
Complete as for right front from **.

BACK
With 3¾ mm (UK 9/US 5) needles, cast on 102 sts.
Beg with a k row, work in st st until back meas 17 cm (6½ in) from
cast-on edge, ending with a RS row.
Next row: P2, p2tog, *p3tog, (p2tog) twice, p2, (p2tog) twice, rep
from * to last 7 sts, p3tog, p2tog, p2. 56 sts.
Change to 3¼ mm (UK 10/US 3) needles.
Next row: (K1, p1) to end.
This row forms moss st.
Rep last row 5 times.

Change to 3¾ mm (UK 9/US 5) needles.
Beg with a k row, cont in st st as follows:
Work 2 rows.

Shape armholes
Cast off 3 sts at beg of next 2 rows. 50 sts.
Dec 1 st at each end of next and foll 2 alt rows. 44 sts.
Cont straight until back matches fronts to start of shoulder shaping,
ending with a WS row.

Shape shoulders
Cast off 7 sts at beg of next 4 rows.
Leave rem 16 sts on holder for back neck.

SLEEVES
With 3¾ mm (UK 9/US 5) needles, cast on 30 sts.
Beg with a k row, work in st st, inc 1 st at each end of 5th and every
foll 6th row until there are 40 sts.
Cont without further shaping until sleeve meas 13 cm (5 in) from
cast-on edge, ending on a WS row.

Shape top
Cast off 3 sts at beg of next 2 rows. 34 sts.
Dec 1 st at both ends of next and every foll alt row until 20 sts rem,
then on every row until 10 sts rem.
Cast off.

NECK BORDER

Join shoulder seams.

With 3¼ mm (UK 10/US 3) needles and RS facing, slip 7 sts from right front safety pin onto right needle, rejoin yarn and pick up and k 15 sts up right side of neck, k 16 sts from back inc 2 sts evenly, pick up and k 15 sts down left side of neck, then patt across 7 sts left on left front safety pin. 62 sts.

Keeping moss st correct as set by front neck sts, proceed as follows:
Work 1 row.

Buttonhole row (RS): Moss st 2, yrn, p2tog, moss st to end.

Work 3 rows.

Cast off loosely in moss st.

CUFF EDGINGS (make 2)

With 3¼ mm (UK 10/US 3) needles, cast on 4 sts.

1st row (RS): K2, yfwd, k2.
2nd row: Sl 1, k4.
3rd row: K3, yfwd, k2.
4th row: Sl 1, k5.
5th row: K2, yfwd, k2tog, yfwd, k2.

6th row: Sl 1, k6.
7th row: K3, yfwd, k2tog, yfwd, k2.
8th row: Cast off 4 sts, k to end. 4 sts.

These 8 rows form patt.

Cont in patt until edging, when slightly stretched, fits along cast-on edge of sleeve, ending with 8th row.

Cast off.

Sew edgings in position.

HEM EDGING

Join side seams.

With 3¼ mm (UK 10/US 3) needles, cast on 4 sts.

Work in patt as for cuff edgings until strip, when slightly stretched, fits along entire cast-on edge of fronts and back, ending with 8th row.

Cast off.

Sew edging in position.

TO MAKE UP

Join sleeve seams. Insert sleeves. Sew on buttons.

STRIPED ROMPER SUIT

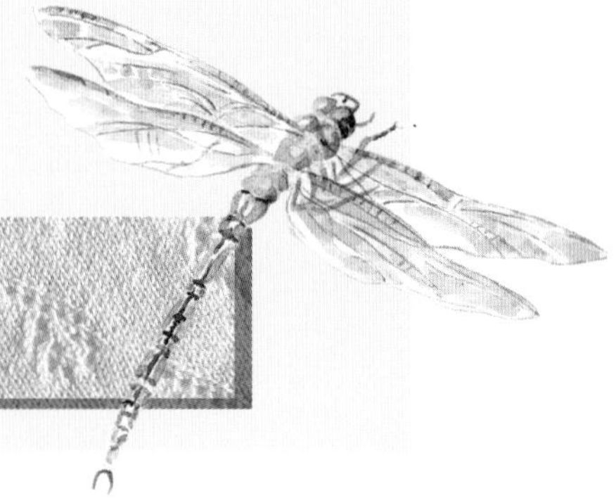

A PRACTICAL AND COMFORTABLE ALL-IN-ONE ROMPER SUIT.

MATERIALS

2 [2, 3] x 50 g balls of Jaeger Matchmaker Merino 4 ply in
A (cream)
2 [2, 3] x 50 g balls of same yarn in B (grey)
Pair each of 2¾ mm (UK 12/US 2) and 3¼ mm (UK 10/US 3)
knitting needles
7 buttons

MEASUREMENTS

To fit age	0–6	6–12	12–18 months
Actual measurement	61	69	78 cm
	24	27¼	30½ in
Length	51	57	64 cm
	20	22½	25¼ in
Sleeve seam	17	18	19 cm
	6½	7	7½ in

ABBREVIATIONS

See page 20.

TENSION

28 sts and 36 rows to 10 cm (4 in) measured over st st using
3¼ mm (UK 10/US 3) needles.

BACK

First leg

With 2¾ mm (UK 12/US 2) needles and A, cast on 33 [39, 45] sts.
1st row (RS): K1, (p1, k1) to end.
This row forms moss st.
Work a further 5 rows in moss st.
Change to 3¼ mm (UK 10/US 3) needles and work in patt as
follows:
1st row (RS): With A, knit.
2nd row: With A, purl.
3rd row: With B, knit.
4th row: With B, purl.
These 4 rows form patt.
Keeping patt correct, proceed as follows:
Work 8 [12, 16] rows.

Shape inside leg

Inc 1 st at beg (inside leg edge) of next and every foll 4th row until
there are 39 [45, 51] sts.
Cont straight until work meas 14 [16, 19] cm (5½ [6¼, 7½] in) from

cast-on edge, ending with a WS row.**
Break yarns and leave sts on a holder.

Second leg

Work as for first leg to **, working inside leg increases at ends of
rows and casting on 7 sts at beg of last row. 46 [52, 58] sts.

Join legs

Next row (RS): K across 46 [52, 58] sts of second leg, then k across
39 [45, 51] sts of first leg. 85 [97, 109] sts.***
Cont in patt until work meas 41 [46, 52] cm (16 [18, 20½] in) from
cast-on edge, ending with a WS row.

Shape armholes

Keeping patt correct, cast off 4 sts at beg of next 2 rows.
77 [89, 101] sts.
Cont straight until work meas 51 [57, 64] cm (20 [22½, 25¼] in)
from cast-on edge, ending with a WS row.
Place markers at each end of last row.

Shape neck

Next row (RS): Patt 28 [33, 38] sts, turn and work this side first.
Cast off 3 [4, 5] sts at beg (neck edge) of next and foll 2 alt rows,
then 2 sts at beg of foll 5 alt rows. 9 [11, 13] sts.
Dec 1 st at neck edge on next 4 [5, 6] rows. 5 [6, 7] sts.
Cast off.
With RS facing, rejoin yarn to rem sts, cast off centre 21 [23, 25] sts,
patt to end.
Work 1 row.
Complete to match first side, reversing shapings.

FRONT

Work as back to ***.
Work 15 rows.

Divide for front opening

Next row (RS): Patt 40 [46, 52] sts, (k1, p1) twice, k1, turn and
work this side first.
Next row: (K1, p1) twice, k1, patt to end.
Keeping patt correct and working front opening edge 5 sts in moss
st as now set, cont straight until front matches back to start of
armhole shaping, ending with a WS row.

Shape armhole

Cast off 4 sts at beg of next row. 41 [47, 53] sts.
Cont straight until front meas 47 [53, 60] cm (18½ [20¾, 23½] in)
from cast-on edge, ending with a RS row.

Shape neck

Cast off 8 sts at beg of next row, then 2 sts at beg of foll 2 alt rows.
29 [35, 41] sts.
Dec 1 st at neck edge on every row until 28 [33, 38] sts rem.
Cont straight until front matches back to markers, ending with a
WS row.
Cast off.

With RS facing, rejoin yarns to rem 40 [46, 52] sts and cont in patt until front matches back to start of armhole shaping, ending with a RS row.

Shape armhole

Cast off 4 sts at beg of next row. 36 [42, 48] sts.

Cont straight until front meas 47 [53, 60] cm (18½ [20¾, 23½] in) from cast-on edge, ending with a WS row.

Shape neck

Cast off 3 sts at beg of next row, then 2 sts at beg of foll 2 alt rows. 29 [35, 41] sts.

Dec 1 st at neck edge on every row until 28 [33, 38] sts rem.

Cont straight until front matches back to markers, ending with a WS row.

Cast off.

SLEEVES

With 2¾ mm (UK 12/US 2) needles and A, cast on 43 [49, 55] sts. Work 6 rows in moss st as for back.

Change to 3¼ mm (UK 10/US 3) needles and work in patt as for back, inc 1 st at each end of 3rd and every foll 5th [6th, 7th] row until there are 59 [63, 69] sts.

Cont straight until sleeve meas 17 [18, 19] cm (6½ [7, 7½] in) from cast-on edge, ending with a WS row.

Cast off.

LEFT FRONT BORDER

With RS facing, 2¾ mm (UK 12/US 2) needles and A, pick up and k 23 [25, 27] sts down left side of neck, from shoulder cast-off to front opening edge.

Beg with a p row, work 3 rows in st st.

Picot row (RS): K1, (yfwd, k2tog) to end.
Work in st st for a further 3 rows.
Cast off.
Fold border in half to inside along picot row and slip stitch in place.

RIGHT FRONT BORDER

With RS facing, 2¾ mm (UK 12/US 2) needles and A, pick up and k 64 [70, 76] sts up right front opening edge from base of front opening to start of neck shaping.
Purl 1 row.
Buttonhole row (RS): K4, *yfwd, k2tog, k7 [8, 9], rep from * to last 6 sts, yfwd, k2tog, k4, then pick up and k 19 [21, 23] sts up right side of neck to shoulder cast-off. 83 [91, 99] sts.
Beg with a p row, work 3 rows in st st.
Picot row (RS): K1, (yfwd, k2tog) to end.
Work in st st for a further 2 rows.
Next row (WS): Cast off 19 [21, 23] sts, p to end. 64 [70, 76] sts.
Work in st st for a further 2 rows.
Buttonhole row (RS): K4, *yfwd, k2tog, k7 [8, 9], rep from * to last 6 sts, yfwd, k2tog, k4.
Purl one row.

Cast off.
Fold border in half to inside along picot row and slip stitch in place, carefully matching buttonholes.

BACK NECK BORDER

With RS facing, 2¾ mm (UK 12/US 2) needles and A, pick up and k 99 [103, 107] sts across entire back neck edge.
Beg with a p row, work 3 rows in st st.
Picot row (RS): K1, (yfwd, k2tog) to end.
Work in st st for a further 3 rows.
Cast off.
Fold border in half to inside along picot row and slip stitch in place.

TO MAKE UP

Matching shoulder cast-off edge of fronts to markers on back, sew fronts under neck shaping to form shoulder seams. Sew neatly in position at side edges. Join side seams. Join sleeve seams. Matching centre of cast-off edge of sleeves to shoulder seams and underarm seams, sew sleeves to back and front. Sew inside leg and crotch seam. Lay right front border over left front moss st border and sew in place at base of opening. Sew on buttons.

PICOT EDGE CARDIGAN
AND BOOTIES

THIS OUTFIT WILL SOON BECOME A FAVOURITE. KNITTED IN
LUXURIOUS CASHMERE, IT HAS A DECORATIVE EDGING WHICH
WILL LOOK LOVELY ON A BOY OR GIRL.

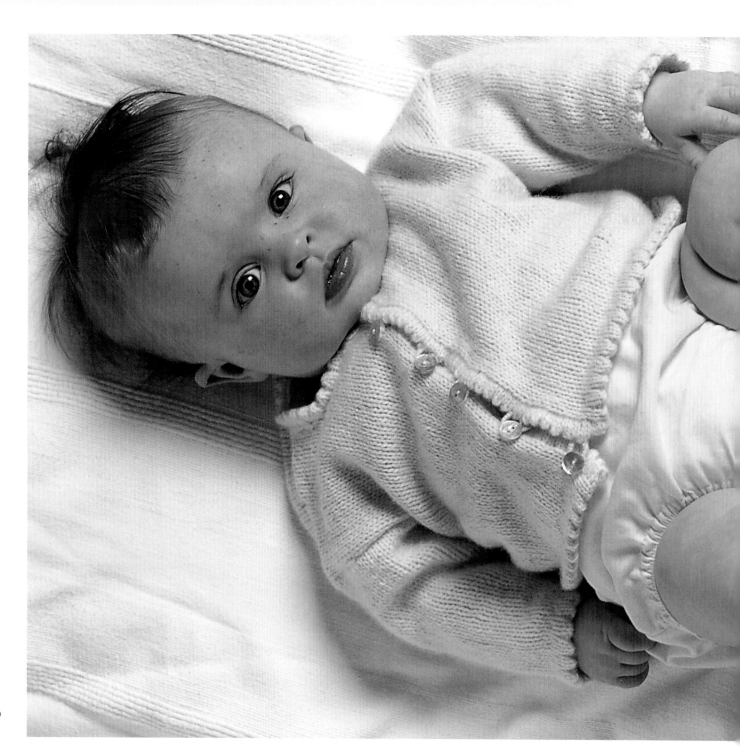

CARDIGAN

BACK

With 2¾ mm (UK 12/US 2) needles cast on 81 [89, 97] sts.
**Beg with a k row, work 4 rows in st st.
Next row (RS) (picot row): K2, (yfwd, k2tog) to last st, k1.
Beg with a p row, work a further 4 rows in st st.**
Change to 3¼ mm (UK 10/US 3) needles.
Beg with a p row, cont in st st until back meas 15 [17, 19] cm
(6 [6½, 7½] in) from picot row, ending with a WS row.

Shape armholes

Cast off 6 sts at beg of next 2 rows. 69 [77, 85] sts.

Work straight until back meas 25 [28, 31] cm (9¾ [11, 12¼] in)
from picot row, ending with a WS row.

Shape shoulders

Cast off 11 [12, 13] sts at beg of next 4 rows.
Leave rem 25 [29, 33] sts on a holder for back neck.

LEFT FRONT

With 2¾ mm (UK 12/US 2) needles cast on 41 [45, 49] sts.
Work from ** to ** as for back.
Change to 3¼ mm (UK 10/US 3) needles.
Beg with a p row, cont in st st until left front matches back to start
of armhole shaping, ending with a WS row.

MATERIALS

4 [5, 6] x 25 g balls of Jaeger Cashmere 4 ply in cream
Pair each of 2¾ mm (UK 12/US 2) and 3¼ mm (UK 10/US 3)
knitting needles
6 buttons

MEASUREMENTS

Cardigan

To fit age	6	12	18 months
Actual measurement	58	64	69 cm
	22¾	25¼	27 in
Length	25	28	31 cm
	9¾	11	12¼ in
Sleeve seam	14	17	20 cm
	5½	6½	7¾ in

Booties

One size to fit age 3–12 months

ABBREVIATIONS

See page 20.

TENSION

28 sts and 36 rows to 10 cm (4 in) measured over st st using
3¼ mm (UK 10/US 3) needles.

Shape armhole

Cast off 6 sts at beg of next row. 35 [39, 43] sts.
Work straight until left front meas 20 [23, 26] cm (7¾ [9, 10¼] in) from picot row, ending with a RS row.

Shape neck

Cast off 6 [7, 8] sts at beg of next row. 29 [32, 35] sts.
Dec 1 st at neck edge of every row until 22 [24, 26] sts rem.
Work straight until left front matches back to shoulders, ending at armhole edge.

Shape shoulder

Cast off 11 [12, 13] sts at beg of next row.
Work 1 row.
Cast off rem 11 [12, 13] sts.

RIGHT FRONT

Work as for left front, reversing all shapings.

SLEEVES

With 2¾ mm (UK 12/US 2) needles cast on 31 [35, 39] sts.
Work from ** to ** as for back.
Change to 3¼ mm (UK 10/US 3) needles.
Beg with a p row, cont in st st, inc 1 st at each end of 2nd and every foll 3rd [4th, 5th] row to 59 [63, 67] sts.
Cont straight until sleeve meas 16 [19, 22] cm (6¼ [7½, 8½] in) from picot edge, ending with a WS row.
Cast off.

NECK BORDER

Join shoulder seams.
With RS and 2¾ mm (UK 12/US 2) needles, pick up and k 22 [23, 24] sts up right side of neck, k 25 [29, 33] sts from back, and pick up and k 22 [23, 24] sts down left side of neck. 69 [75, 81] sts.
***Beg with a p row, work 3 rows in st st.

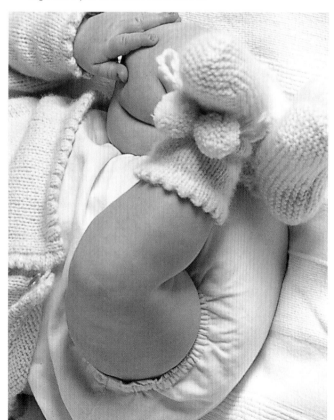

Next row (RS) (picot row): K1, (yfwd, k2tog) to end.
Beg with a p row, work a further 3 rows in st st.
Cast off loosely.***

FRONT BORDERS (both alike)

With RS facing and 2¾ mm (UK 12/US 2) needles pick up and k 69 [79, 89] sts evenly along one front opening edge between picot row of neck border and picot row of hem.
Work as for neck border from *** to ***.

TO MAKE UP

Mark points along row end edges of sleeves 2 cm (¾ in) below cast-off edge. Matching centre of cast-off edge of sleeves to shoulders and markers to top of side seams, sew sleeves to back and fronts. Join side and sleeve seams. Fold all borders to inside along picot rows and slip stitch in place to form picot edging.
Attach 6 buttons to left front, placing buttons over front border pick-up row – position top button level with neck border pick-up row, lowest button 2 cm (¾ in) up from lower picot row and rem 4 buttons evenly spaced between. Make button loops along right front opening edge to correspond with buttons.

BOOTIES (make 2)

With 2¾ mm (UK 12/US 2) needles cast on 39 sts.
Beg with a k row, work 4 rows st st.
Next row (RS) (picot row): K2, (yfwd, k2tog) to last st, k1.
Beg with a p row, work a further 5 rows in st st.
Change to 3¼ mm (UK 10/US 3) needles.
Cont in st st as follows:
Work 20 rows.

Shape ankle

1st row (RS): K7, k2tog, (k8, k2tog) to end. 35 sts.
2nd row: K1, (p1, k1) to end.
3rd row: P1, (k1, p1) to end.
4th row: K1, (yfwd, k2tog) to end.
5th row: As 3rd row.
6th row: As 2nd row.

Shape instep

Next row (RS): K23, turn.
Next row: P11, turn.
Knit 24 rows on these 11 sts.
Break off yarn.
With RS facing, rejoin yarn at end of first set of 12 sts, pick up and k 15 sts along first side of instep, k 11 instep sts, then pick up and k 15 sts along second side of instep, k rem 12 sts. 65 sts.
Knit 9 rows.

Shape sole

1st row (RS): K2tog, k29, k3tog, k29, k2tog.
2nd row: Knit.
3rd row: K2tog, k27, k3tog, k27, k2tog.
4th row: Knit.
5th row: K2tog, k25, k3tog, k25, k2tog.
6th row: Knit.
Cast off rem 53 sts.

TO MAKE UP

Join back and sole seams. Fold cast-on edge to inside along picot row and slip stitch in position. Make 2 twisted cords about 38 cm (15 in) long and thread in and out of eyelet row at ankle. Make 4 small pompoms and attach to ends of twisted cords.

FAIR ISLE JACKET

THIS RAGLAN SLEEVED JACKET IS SMART WITH A TRADITIONAL FEEL.

BACK

With 2¾ mm (UK 12/US 2) needles and A, cast on 109 sts.

1st row (RS): K1, (p1, k1) to end.

This row forms moss st.

Work a further 5 rows in moss st.

Change to 3¼ mm (UK 10/US 3) needles and, beg with a k row, work in st st for 2 rows.

Now work 15 rows in Fair Isle patt following chart on page 67.

Break off all contrasts and cont using A only.

Beg with a p row, cont in st st until back meas 20 cm (7¾ in), ending with a WS row.

Next row (RS): K1, (k2tog, k3) 21 times, k2tog, k1. 87 sts.

Change to 2¾ mm (UK 12/US 2) needles and work in moss st for

5 rows.

Change to 3¼ mm (UK 10/US 3) needles.

Next row (RS): K2tog, (k4, k2tog) 14 times, k1. 72 sts.

Next row: Purl.

Shape raglan armholes

Cast off 5 sts at beg of next 2 rows. 62 sts.

1st row (RS): K1, k2tog tbl, k to last 3 sts, k2tog, k1.

2nd row: Purl.

Rep last 2 rows until 24 sts remain, ending with a WS row.

Cast off.

LEFT FRONT

With 2¾ mm (UK 12/US 2) needles and A, cast on 63 sts.

Work 6 rows in moss stitch as for back.

Change to 3¼ mm (UK 10/US 3) needles.

1st row (RS): K to last 7 sts, moss st 7.

2nd row: Moss st 7, p to end.

These 2 rows form patt – front opening edge 7 sts still worked in moss st with all other sts now worked in st st.

3rd row: Work first 56 sts in Fair Isle patt following chart, using A moss st 7.

4th row: Using A moss st 7, work last 56 sts in Fair Isle patt.

Cont in this way until all 15 rows of chart have been worked.

Break off all contrasts and cont using A only.

Beg with a WS row, cont in patt until left front meas 20 cm (7¾ in), ending with a WS row.

Next row (RS): (K2tog, k3) 11 times, k2tog, moss st 6. 51 sts.

Change to 2¾ mm (UK 12/US 2) needles and work in moss st for 5 rows.

Change to 3¼ mm (UK 10/US 3) needles.

Next row (RS): K6, k2tog, (k2, k2tog) 9 times, moss st 7. 41 sts.

Next row: Moss st 7, p to end.

Shape raglan armhole

Cast off 5 sts at beg of next row. 36 sts.

1st row (WS): Moss st 7, p to end.

2nd row: K1, k2tog tbl, k to last 7 sts, moss st 7.

Rep last 2 rows until 22 sts rem, ending with a RS row.

Shape neck

Cast off 9 sts at beg of next row. 13 sts.

Working raglan decreases in same way as for back, dec 1 st at both ends of next and every foll alt row until 3 sts rem.

Now dec 1 st at raglan edge only on foll alt row. 2 sts.

Work 1 row, thus ending with a p row.

Next row (RS): K2tog and fasten off.

Mark positions for 3 buttons along front opening edge border – top button 1 cm (⅜ in) below neck shaping, lowest button level with last row of moss st across body and rem button evenly spaced between.

MATERIALS

3 x 50 g balls of Rowan True 4 ply Botany in A (light blue)
1 ball of same yarn in each of B (dark blue), C (white),
D (purple), E (dusky pink) and F (pink)
Pair each of 2¾ mm (UK 12/US 2) and 3¼ mm (UK 10/US 3)
knitting needles
3 buttons

MEASUREMENTS

To fit age	3–9 months
Actual measurement (at underarm)	51 cm
	20 in
Length	34 cm
	13½ in
Sleeve seam	14 cm
	5½ in

ABBREVIATIONS

See page 20.

TENSION

28 sts and 36 rows to l0 cm (4 in) measured over st st using 3¼ mm (UK 10/US 3) knitting needles.

NOTE

When working Fair Isle patt from chart, read chart from right to left on RS k rows and from left to right on WS p rows. Beg and end rows at points indicated and rep the 12 st patt repeat as required across rows. Strand yarn not in use loosely across WS of work to keep fabric elastic.

RIGHT FRONT

Work as for left front reversing all shapings and with the addition of 3 buttonholes worked to correspond with positions marked for buttons as follows:

Buttonhole row (RS): Moss st 2, k2tog, yfwd, moss st 3, k to end.

SLEEVES

With 2¾ mm (UK 12/US 2) needles and A, cast on 39 sts.
Work 6 rows in moss st as for back.
Change to 3¼ mm (UK 10/US 3) needles.
Beg with a k row, work in st st for 2 rows.
Now work in Fair Isle patt following chart until all 15 rows have been worked *and at the same time* inc 1 st at each end of 3rd and every foll 6th row. 45 sts.
Break off all contrasts and cont using A only.
Beg with a p row, cont in st st, inc 1 st at each end of every foll 6th row from previous inc until there are 51 sts.
Cont straight until sleeve meas 14 cm (5½ in), ending with a WS row.

Shape raglan

Cast off 5 sts at beg of next 2 rows. 41 sts.
Working all decreases in same way as for back, dec 1 st at each end of next and every foll 4th row until 31 sts rem, then on every foll alt row until 9 sts rem.

Work 1 row, thus ending with a WS row.
Cast off.

COLLAR

With 2¾ mm (UK 12/US 2) needles and A, cast on 85 sts.
Work in moss st as for back for 6 rows.
Change to 3¼ mm (UK 10/US 3) needles and cont as follows:

Next row (RS): Moss st 4, k to last 4 sts, moss st 4.
Next row: Moss st 4, p to last 4 sts, moss st 4.
These 2 rows form patt – edge 4 sts still worked in moss st with all other sts now worked in st st.

3rd row: Using A moss st 4, work next 77 sts in Fair Isle patt following chart, using A moss st 4.
4th row: Using A moss st 4, work next 77 sts in Fair Isle patt, using A moss st 4.
Cont in this way until all 15 rows of chart have been worked.
Break off all contrasts and cont using A only.
Work a further 6 rows in patt.
Cast off.

TO MAKE UP

Join front and back raglan seams. Join side and sleeve seams. Sew cast-off edge of collar to neck edge, positioning ends of collar 3 sts in from front opening edges. Sew on buttons.

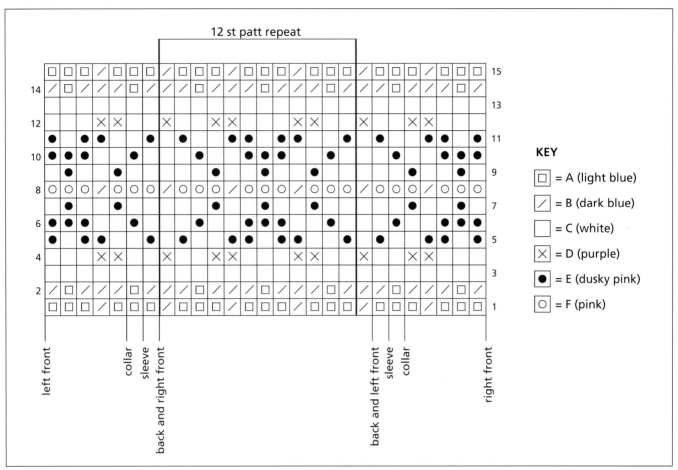

12 st patt repeat

KEY

☐	= A (light blue)
⁄	= B (dark blue)
☐	= C (white)
✕	= D (purple)
●	= E (dusky pink)
○	= F (pink)

FAIR ISLE TWINSET

KEEP TRADITIONS ALIVE WITH FAIR ISLE. THIS TWINSET IS KNITTED IN GREY, PINK AND MUTED COLOURS.

MATERIALS

Cardigan
3 x 50 g balls of Jaeger Matchmaker Merino 4 ply (or Rowan True 4 ply Botany) in A (grey)
1 ball of same yarn in each of B (deep pink), C (light pink), D (light blue), E (buttermilk) and F (heather)
7 buttons

Sweater
2 x 50 g balls of Jaeger Matchmaker Merino 4 ply (or Rowan True 4 ply Botany) in A (grey)
Small amounts of same yarn in each of B (deep pink), C (light pink), D (light blue), E (buttermilk) and F (heather)
3 buttons

Cardigan or Sweater
Pair each of 2¾ mm (UK 12/US 2) and 3¼ mm (UK 10/US 3) knitting needles

MEASUREMENTS

To fit age	12–18 months
Cardigan	
Actual measurement	62 cm
	24¼ in
Length	30 cm
	11¾ in
Sleeve seam	23 cm
	9 in
Sweater	
Actual measurement	56 cm
	22¼ in
Length	28 cm
	11 in
Sleeve seam	7 cm
	2¾ in

ABBREVIATIONS
See page 20.

TENSION
Cardigan: 32 sts and 32 rows to 10 cm (4 in) measured over Fair Isle patt using 3¼ mm (UK 10/US 3) knitting needles.
Sweater: 28 sts and 36 rows to 10 cm (4 in) measured over st st using 3¼ mm (UK 10/US 3) knitting needles.

NOTE
When working Fair Isle patt from chart, read chart from right to left on RS k rows and from left to right on WS p rows.

CARDIGAN

BACK
With 2¾ mm (UK 12/US 2) needles and B, cast on 89 sts.
Break off B and join in A.
1st row (RS): K1, (p1, k1) to end.
2nd row: P1, (k1, p1) to end.
These 2 rows form rib.
Work a further 7 rows in rib.
Next row (WS): Rib 3, inc in next st, (rib 8, inc in next st) 9 times, rib 4. 99 sts.
Change to 3¼ mm (UK 10/US 3) needles.
Beg with a k row, now work in st st following chart on page 70 – beg and end rows as indicated, read odd numbered k rows from right to left and even numbered p rows from left to right and rep the 42 rows patt rep as required.
Keeping patt correct, cont until back meas 17 cm (6½ in) from cast-on edge, ending with a WS row.

Shape armholes
Keeping patt correct, cast off 2 sts at beg of next 10 rows. 79 sts.
Cont straight until back meas 30 cm (11¾ in) from cast-on edge, ending with a WS row.

Shape shoulders
Cast off 11 sts at beg of next 4 rows.
Leave rem 35 sts on a holder for back neck.

LEFT FRONT
With 2¾ mm (UK 12/US 2) needles and B, cast on 45 sts.
Break off B and join in A.
Work 9 rows in rib as for back.
Next row (WS): Rib 4, inc in next st, (rib 8, inc in next st) 4 times, rib 4. 50 sts.
Change to 3¼ mm (UK 10/US 3) needles.
Beg with a k row, now work in st st following chart until left front matches back to start of armhole shaping, ending with a WS row.

Shape armhole
Keeping patt correct, cast off 2 sts at beg of next and foll 4 alt rows. 40 sts.
Cont straight until left front meas 26 cm (10¼ in) from cast-on edge, ending with a RS row.

Shape neck
Next row (WS): Patt 8 sts and slip these 8 sts onto a safety pin, patt to end. 32 sts.
Work 1 row.
Cast off 4 sts at beg of next row, and 2 sts at beg of foll alt row. 26 sts.
Dec 1 st at neck edge on every row until 22 sts rem.

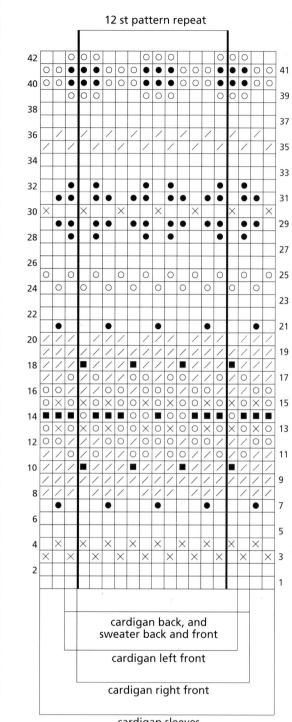

12 st pattern repeat

cardigan back, and
sweater back and front

cardigan left front

cardigan right front

cardigan sleeves

KEY

☐ = A (grey)

● = B (deep pink)

⁄ = C (light pink)

○ = D (light blue)

✕ = E (buttermilk)

■ = F (heather)

Cont straight until left
front matches back to start of
shoulder shaping, ending with a WS row.

Shape shoulder
Cast off 11 sts at beg of next row.
Work 1 row.
Cast off rem 11 sts.

RIGHT FRONT
Work to match left front, reversing all shapings.

SLEEVES
With 2¾ mm (UK 12/US 2) needles and B, cast on 49 sts.
Break off B and join in A.
Work 11 rows in rib as for back.
Next row (WS): Rib 4, inc in next st, (rib 7, inc in next st) 5 times,
rib 4. 55 sts.
Change to 3¼ mm (UK 10/US 3) needles.
Beg with a k row, now work in st st following chart, inc 1 st at each
end of 3rd and every foll 4th row until there are 85 sts, taking inc sts
into patt.
Cont straight until sleeve meas 23 cm (9 in) from cast-on edge,
ending with a WS row.
Shape top
Cast off 2 sts at beg of next 10 rows.
Cast off rem 65 sts.

NECK BORDER
Join shoulder seams.
With 2¾ mm (UK 12/US 2) needles, A and RS facing, k 8 sts left on
right front safety pin, pick up and k 14 sts up right side of neck,
k 35 sts from back, pick up and k 14 sts down left side of neck, then
k 8 sts left on left front safety pin. 79 sts.
Beg with 2nd row, work in rib as for back for 7 rows.
Break off A and join in B.
Cast off in rib.

BUTTONHOLE BORDER
With 2¾ mm (UK 12/US 2) needles, A and RS facing, pick up and
k 81 sts along right front opening edge, between cast-on edge and
top of neck border.
Beg with 2nd row, work 2 rows in rib as for back.
Next row (RS): Rib 3, (cast off 2 sts, rib until there are 10 sts on right
needle after cast-off) 6 times, cast off 2 sts, rib to end.
Next row: Rib to end, casting on 2 sts over those cast off on
previous row. Work a further 3 rows in rib.

Break off A and join in B.
Cast off in rib.

BUTTON BORDER
Work to match buttonhole border, omitting buttonholes.

TO MAKE UP
Join side seams. Join sleeve seams. Insert sleeves. Sew on buttons.

SWEATER

BACK
With 2¾ mm (UK 12/US 2) needles and B, cast on 79 sts.
Break off B and join in A.
Work 10 rows in rib as for back.
Change to 3¼ mm (UK 10/US 3) needles.
Beg with a k row, now work in st st until back meas 16 cm (6¼ in) from cast-on edge, ending with a WS row.

Shape armholes
Cast off 2 sts at beg of next 8 rows. 63 sts.
Work 2 rows.
Beg with a k row, now work chart rows 7 to 15 (see page 70) – beg and end rows as indicated, read odd numbered k rows from right to left and even numbered p rows from left to right. (15 patt rows completed.)
Cont in st st using A only as follows:
Work 3 rows.**

Divide for back opening
Next row (RS): K29, turn and work this side first.
Cont straight until back meas 28 cm (11 in) from cast-on edge, ending at armhole edge.

Shape shoulder
Cast off 8 sts at beg of next and foll alt row.
Leave rem 13 sts on a holder.
With RS facing, slip centre 5 sts onto a safety pin, rejoin yarn to rem sts and k to end. Complete to match first side.

FRONT
Work as for back to **.

Shape neck
Next row (RS): K23, turn and work this side first.
Dec 1 st at neck edge of every row until 16 sts rem.

Cont straight until front matches back to start of shoulder shaping, ending at armhole edge.

Shape shoulder
Cast off 8 sts at beg of next row.
Work 1 row.
Cast off rem 8 sts.
With RS facing, slip centre 17 sts onto a holder, rejoin yarn to rem sts, k to end. Complete to match first side, reversing shapings.

SLEEVES
With 2¾ mm (UK 12/US 2) needles and B, cast on 59 sts.
Break off B and join in A.
Work 4 rows in rib as for back.
Change to 3¼ mm (UK 10/US 3) needles.
Beg with a k row, now work in st st, inc 1 st at each end of 3rd and every foll 3rd row until there are 71 sts.
Cont straight until sleeve meas 7 cm (2¾ in) from cast-on edge, ending with a WS row.

Shape top
Cast off 2 sts at beg of next 8 rows.
Cast off rem 55 sts.

BUTTON BORDER
With 2¾ mm (UK 12/US 2) needles and A, cast on 7 sts.
1st row (RS): P1, (k1, p1) twice, k2.
2nd row: K1, (p1, k1) 3 times.
Rep last 2 rows 8 times more.
Break yarn and leave these 7 sts on a safety pin.

BUTTONHOLE BORDER
With 2¾ mm (UK 12/US 2) needles, A and RS facing, rejoin yarn to sts at base of back opening and proceed as follows:
1st row (RS): K1, inc in next st, k2, inc in next st. 7 sts.
2nd row: K1, (p1, k1) 3 times.
3rd row: K2, (p1, k1) twice, p1.
Last 2 rows form rib.
Work a further 1 row in rib.
Buttonhole row (RS): Rib 3, yrn, p2tog, rib 2.
Work 7 rows.
Rep buttonhole row once more.
Work 5 rows.
Do NOT break yarn and leave sts on needle.

NECKBAND
Join shoulder seams. Sew buttonhole border to left side of opening and button border to right side. Sew cast-on edge of button border in place on inside at base of opening.
With 2¾ mm (UK 12/US 2) needles, RS facing and A, rib across first 6 sts of buttonhole border, k tog last st of buttonhole border with first st left on left back holder, k rem 12 sts, pick up and k 14 sts down left side of neck, k 17 sts from front neck, pick up and k 14 sts up right side of neck, k first 12 sts left on right back holder, k tog last st of back neck with first st of button border, rib across rem 6 sts. 81 sts.
Work 5 rows in rib as set, making 3rd buttonhole in same way as before in 2nd of these rows.
Break off A and join in B.
Cast off in rib.

TO MAKE UP
Join side seams. Join sleeve seams. Insert sleeves. Sew on buttons.

HOODED MOSS STITCH JACKET

THIS BEAUTIFULLY WARM, HOODED JACKET WITH POCKETS IS EASY TO KNIT IN A FLECKED, CHUNKY WEIGHT YARN.

MATERIALS

3 [4, 4] x 100 g hanks of Rowan Magpie Tweed in heather
Pair each of 4½ mm (UK 7/US 7) and 5 mm (UK 6/US 8) knitting needles
5 buttons

MEASUREMENTS

To fit age	6–12	12–18	18–24 months
Actual measurement	68	70	74 cm
	26¾	27½	29 in
Length	30	35	39 cm
	11¾	13¾	15¼ in
Sleeve seam	19	21	23 cm
	7½	8¼	9 in

ABBREVIATIONS

See page 20.

TENSION

18 sts and 32 rows to l0 cm (4 in) measured over moss stitch using 5 mm (UK 6/US 8) needles.

BACK

With 5 mm (UK 6/US 8) needles cast on 61 [63, 67] sts.
1st row: K1, (p1, k1) to end.
This row forms moss st.
Cont in moss st until back meas 30 [35, 39] cm (11¾ [13¾, 15¼] in) from cast-on edge, ending with a WS row.
Shape shoulders
Cast off 10 [10, 11] sts at beg of next 2 rows, and 10 [11, 11] sts at beg of foll 2 rows.
Leave rem 21 [21, 23] sts on a st holder for back neck.

RIGHT FRONT

With 5 mm (UK 6/US 8) needles cast on 29 [31, 33] sts.

Work 5 [5, 6] cm (2 [2, 2½] in) in moss st as for back, ending with a WS row.

Buttonhole row (RS): Moss st 2, cast off 2 sts, moss st to end.

Next row: Moss st to end, casting on 2 sts over those cast off on previous row.

Cont straight for a further 5.5 [6.5, 7] cm (2 [2½, 2¾] in), ending with a WS row.**

Rep from ** to ** twice more.

Work straight until right front meas 26 [30, 33] cm (10¼ [11¾, 13] in), ending with WS row.

Shape neck

Cast off 4 sts at beg of next row. 25 [27, 29] sts.

Dec 1 st at neck edge on next 5 [6, 7] rows. 20 [21, 22] sts.

Cont straight until right front matches back to start of shoulder shaping, ending with a RS row.

Shape shoulder

Cast off 10 [10, 11] sts at beg of next row.

Work 1 row.

Cast off rem 10 [11, 11] sts.

LEFT FRONT

Work as for right front, omitting buttonholes and reversing all shapings.

SLEEVES

With 5 mm (UK 6/US 8) needles, cast on 31 [33, 35] sts.

Work 14 rows in moss st as for back.

Change to 4½ mm (UK 7/US 7) needles and work a further 14 rows.

Change to 5 mm (UK 6/US 8) needles and cont in moss st, inc 1 st at each end of next and every foll 3rd [4th, 4th] row until there are 53 [55, 59] sts.

Cont without further shaping until sleeve meas 23 [25, 27] cm (9 [9¾, 10½] in) from cast-on edge, ending with a WS row.

Cast off.

HOOD

Join shoulder seams.

With 5 mm (UK 6/US 8) needles and RS facing, starting and ending at front opening edges, pick up and knit 16 sts up right side of neck, patt across 21 [21, 23] sts left on back neck st holder, then pick up and knit 16 sts down left side of neck. 53 [53, 55] sts.

Work 3 rows in moss st, then rep the 2 buttonhole rows once more.

Cast off 4 sts at beg of next 2 rows. 45 [45, 47] sts.

Next row (RS): Moss st 7 [3, 5], *inc once in each of next 2 sts,

moss st 4 [4, 3], rep from * to last 2 [0, 2] sts, moss st 2 [0, 2].
57 [59, 63] sts.
Cont in moss st until hood meas 18 [19, 20] cm (7 [7½, 7¾] in),
from pick-up row.
Cast off.

POCKETS (make 2)
With 5 mm (UK 6/US 8) needles cast on 13 [15, 15] sts.
Work in moss st as for back for 26 [28, 30] rows.
Cast off.

TO MAKE UP
Join shoulder seams. Join top seam of hood. Matching centre of
cast-off edge of sleeves to shoulder seams, sew sleeves to back and
fronts. Join side and sleeve seams, reversing sleeve seam for first
14 rows for turn-back cuff. Attach pockets as in photograph on
page 72. Sew on buttons.

STRIPED TUNIC

ALWAYS A CLASSIC, THIS NAUTICAL TUNIC IS SIMPLE TO KNIT AND
IDEAL FOR BEGINNERS.

MATERIALS

3 [4, 4] x 50 g balls of Rowan Cotton Glace in A (navy)
1 [2, 2] x 50 g balls of same yarn in B (white)
Pair each 2¾ mm (UK 12/US 2) and 3¼ mm (UK 10/US 3)
knitting needles
3 buttons

MEASUREMENTS

To fit age	6	12	24 months
Actual measurement	58	66	74 cm
	22¾	26	29 in
Length	32	37	44 cm
	12½	14½	17¼ in
Sleeve seam	14.5	16.5	19.5 cm
	5¾	6½	7½ in

ABBREVIATIONS

See page 20.

TENSION

25 sts and 34 rows to 10 cm (4 in) measured over st st using
3¼ mm (UK 10/US 3) needles.

BACK

With 2¾ mm (UK 12/US 2) needles and A, cast on 73 [83, 93] sts.
K 5 rows.
Change to 3¼ mm (UK 10/US 3) needles.
Join in B.
1st row (RS): Using A k4, using B k to last 4 sts, using A k4.
2nd row: Using A k4, using B p to last 4 sts, using A k4.
3rd row: Using A knit.
4th row: Using A k4, p to last 4 sts, k4.
5th to 8th rows: As 3rd and 4th rows, twice.
9th and 10th rows: As 1st and 2nd rows.
11th row (RS): Using A knit.
12th row: Using A purl.
13th to 16th rows: as 11th and 12th rows, twice.
17th row: Using B knit.
18th row: Using B purl.
11th to 18th rows form stripe patt and are now repeated.
Work straight until back meas 19 [23, 29] cm (7½ [9, 11½] in) from
cast-on edge, ending with a WS row.
Shape armholes
Keeping patt correct, cast off 4 sts at beg of next 2 rows.
65 [75, 85] sts.
Work straight until armhole meas 13 [14, 15] cm (5 [5½, 6] in),
ending with a WS row.
Shape shoulders
Next row (RS): Cast off first 22 [24, 28] sts for right shoulder, k until
there are 21 [27, 29] sts on right needle and slip these sts onto a
holder for back neck, k to end.
Break yarn and leave rem 22 [24, 28] sts on another holder for left
shoulder.

FRONT

Work as given for back until 18 rows less have been worked than on
back to start of shoulder shaping, thus ending with a WS row.
Shape neck
Next row (RS): K27 [31, 36], turn and work this side first.
Dec 1 st at neck edge on next 5 [7, 8] rows. 22 [24, 28] sts.
Work 12 [10, 9] rows.
Shape shoulder
Break yarn and leave rem 22 [24, 28] sts on a holder for left
shoulder.
With RS facing, slip centre 11 [13, 13] sts onto another holder,
rejoin yarn to rem sts, k to end.
Dec 1 st at neck edge on next 5 [7, 8] rows. 22 [24, 28] sts.
Work 12 [10, 9] rows.
Shape shoulder
Cast off rem 22 [24, 28] sts.

SLEEVES (both alike)

With 2¾ mm (UK 12/US 2) needles and A, cast on 50 [54, 56] sts.
K 6 rows.
Change to 3¼ mm (UK 10/US 3) needles.
Beg with 2 rows using B, now work in stripe patt as for back, inc
1 st at each end of 5th and every foll 5th [6th, 6th] row until there
are 62 [66, 72] sts.
Work straight until sleeve meas 16 [18, 21] cm (6¼ [7, 8¼] in) from
cast-on edge, ending with a WS row.
Cast off.

NECK BORDER

Join right shoulder seam.
With RS facing, 2¾ mm (UK 12/US 2) needles and A, pick up and
k 16 sts down left side of neck, k 11 [13, 13] sts from front, pick up
and k 16 sts up right side of neck, then k 21 [27, 29] sts from back.
64 [72, 74] sts.
Knit 4 rows.
Cast off knitwise.

LEFT FRONT SHOULDER BORDER

With RS facing, 2¾ mm (UK 12/US 2) needles and A, k 22 [24, 28]
sts from left shoulder, then pick up and k 4 sts across end of neck
border. 26 [28, 32] sts.
Knit 1 row.
Buttonhole row (RS): K2, k2tog, yfwd, (k8 [9, 11], k2tog, yfwd)
twice, k2.
Knit 2 rows.
Cast off knitwise.

LEFT BACK SHOULDER BORDER

With RS facing, 2¾ mm (UK 12/US 2) needles and A, pick up and
k 4 sts across end of neck border, then k 22 [24, 28] sts from left
shoulder. 26 [28, 32] sts.
Knit 4 rows.
Cast off knitwise.

TO MAKE UP

Lay front shoulder border over back border so that pick-up rows
match and sew together at armhole edge. Mark points along row
end edges of sleeves 1.5 cm (⅝ in) below cast-off edge. Matching
centre of cast-off edge of sleeves to shoulders and markers to top of
side seams, sew sleeves to back and fronts. Join side and sleeve
seams, leaving side seams open for first 14 rows. Sew on buttons.

SAMPLER SWEATER

THIS SWEATER IS BASED ON THE TRADITIONAL SAMPLER – YOUR
CHILD WILL LOVE COUNTING THE RABBITS, HEARTS AND FLOWERS.

MATERIALS

4 [5] x 50 g balls of Rowan Cotton Glace in A (cream)
Small amounts of same yarn in each of B (blue), C (pink),
D (olive), E (grey), F (black) and G (purple)
Pair each of 3¼ mm (UK 10/US 3) and 3¾ mm (UK 9/US 5)
knitting needles

MEASUREMENTS

To fit age	6–9	18–24 months
Actual measurement	62	75 cm
	24½	29½ in
Length	28	31 cm
	11	12¼ in
Sleeve seam	16	20 cm
	6¼	7¾ in

ABBREVIATIONS

See page 20.

TENSION

26 sts and 32 rows to l0 cm (4 in) measured over patt using
3¾ mm (UK 9/US 5) needles.

NOTE

When working patt from chart, read chart from right to
left on RS k rows and from left to right on WS p rows. Beg
and end rows at points indicated and rep the 16 st patt
repeat as required across rows. Use separate lengths of
yarn for each rabbit and sheep motif, twisting yarns
together where they meet to avoid holes forming.
Elsewhere, strand yarn not in use loosely across WS of
work to keep fabric elastic.

BACK

With 3¼ mm (UK 10/US 3) needles and A, cast on 78 [94] sts.
1st row (RS): K2, (p2, k2) to end.
2nd row: P2, (k2, p2) to end.
Rep last 2 rows 3 times more, inc 3 sts evenly across last row.
81 [97] sts.
Change to 3¾ mm (UK 9/US 4) needles.
Beg with a k row, now work in st st following chart on page 83 –
beg and end rows as indicated, read odd numbered k rows from
right to left and even numbered p rows from left to right and rep
the 56 row patt rep as required.
Keeping patt correct, cont until back meas 28 [31] cm (11 [12¼] in)
from cast-on edge, ending with a WS row.
Shape shoulders
Cast off 13 [16] sts at beg of next 4 rows.
Leave rem 29 [33] sts on a holder for back neck.

FRONT

Work as for back until 20 rows less have been worked than on back to start of shoulder shaping, ending with a WS row.

Shape neck

Next row (RS): Patt 33 [39] sts, turn and work this side first.

Dec 1 st at neck edge on next 5 rows, then on foll 2 alt rows. 26 [32] sts.

Work 10 rows, thus ending at armhole edge.

Shape shoulder

Cast off 13 [16] sts at beg of next row. Work 1 row.

Cast off rem 13 [16] sts.

With RS facing, slip centre 15 [19] sts onto a holder, rejoin yarn to rem sts and patt to end. Complete to match first side.

SLEEVES

With 3¼ mm (UK 10/US 3) needles and A, cast on 42 [46] sts.

Work 7 rows in rib as for back, ending with a RS row.

8th row (WS): Rib 3 [5], m1, (rib 6 [9], m1) 6 [4] times, rib 3 [5]. 49 [51] sts.

Change to 3¾ mm (UK 9/US 4) needles.

Beg with a k row, now work in st st following chart, inc 1 st at each end of 3rd and every 3rd [4th] row until there are 67 [73] sts, working inc sts into patt.

Cont straight until sleeve meas 16 [20] cm (6¼ [7¾] in) from cast-on edge, ending with a WS row.

Cast off.

NECK BORDER

Join right shoulder seam.

With 3¼ mm (UK 10/US 3) needles and A, pick up and k 15 [17] sts down left side of neck, k 15 [19] sts from front, pick up and k 15 [17] sts up right side of neck, k 29 [33] sts from back. 74 [86] sts.

Beg with a 2nd row, work 8 rows in rib as for back.

Beg with a p row, work 6 rows in st st.

Cast off loosely knitwise.

TO MAKE UP

Join left shoulder and neckband seam, reversing seam for st st roll. Matching centre of cast-off edge of sleeves to shoulder seams, sew sleeves to back and front. Join side and sleeve seams.

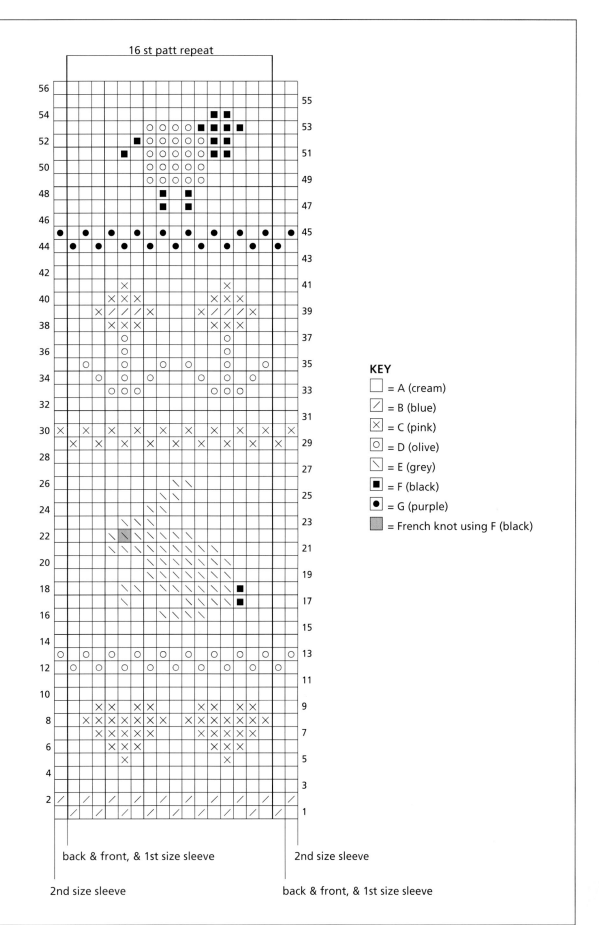

16 st patt repeat

KEY

☐ = A (cream)

◹ = B (blue)

☒ = C (pink)

⊙ = D (olive)

◺ = E (grey)

■ = F (black)

● = G (purple)

▨ = French knot using F (black)

back & front, & 1st size sleeve

2nd size sleeve

2nd size sleeve

back & front, & 1st size sleeve

MOSS STITCH CARDIGAN WITH CABLE EDGING

ADD A TWIST WITH THIS CABLE-EDGED CARDIGAN.

MATERIALS

3 [4, 5] x 50 g balls of Rowan Cotton Glace in pale pink
Pair each of 3 mm (UK 11/US 2/3) and 3¼ mm (UK 10/US 3)
knitting needles
Cable needle
2 buttons

MEASUREMENTS

To fit age	12	18	24 months
Actual measurement	65	70	74 cm
	25½	27½	29 in
Length	25	28	31 cm
	9¾	11	12¼ in
Sleeve seam	17	20	23 cm
	6½	7¾	9 in

ABBREVIATIONS

See page 20.

TENSION

25 sts and 40 rows to l0 cm (4 in) measured over moss st
using 3¼ mm (UK 10/US 3) needles.

BACK

With 3¼ mm (UK 10/US 3) needles, cast on 81 [87, 93] sts.
1st row (RS): K1, (p1, k1) to end.
This row forms moss st.
Cont in moss st until back meas 21 [24, 27] cm (8¼ [9½, 10½] in)
from cast-on edge, ending with a WS row.
Shape back neck
Next row (RS): Patt 28 [30, 32] sts, turn and work this side first.
Dec 1 st at neck edge of next 6 rows. 22 [24, 26] sts.
Work 1 row.
Shape shoulder
Cast off 11 [12, 13] sts at beg of next row.
Work 1 row.
Cast off rem 11 [12, 13] sts.
With RS facing, rejoin yarn to rem sts, cast off 25 [27, 29] sts, patt
to end. 28 [30, 32] sts. Complete to match first side.

LEFT FRONT

With 3¼ mm (UK 10/US 3) needles, cast on 23 [25, 27] sts.
Work 1 row in moss st as for back.
Keeping moss st correct, inc 1 st at beg of next and every foll alt row
until there are 37 [40, 43] sts, taking inc sts into moss st.
Cont straight until left front meas 11 [12, 13] cm (4¼ [4¾, 5] in)
from cast-on edge, ending at straight side seam edge.
Shape front slope
Dec 1 st at end (neck edge) of next row and at same edge on every
foll 3rd row until 22 [24, 26] sts rem.
Cont straight until left front matches back to start of shoulder
shaping, ending at straight side edge.
Shape shoulder
Cast off 11 [12, 13] sts at beg of next row.
Work 1 row.
Cast off rem 11 [12, 13] sts.

RIGHT FRONT

Work to match left front, reversing all shapings.

SLEEVES

With 3 mm (UK 11/US 2/3) needles, cast on 39 [41, 43] sts.
Knit 9 rows.
Change to 3¼ mm (UK 10/US 3) needles.
Now work in moss st as for back, inc 1 st at each end of 3rd and
every foll 6th row until there are 55 [61, 67] sts, taking inc sts into
moss st.
Cont straight until sleeve meas 17 [20, 23] cm (6½ [7¾, 9] in) from
cast-on edge, ending with a WS row.
Cast off.

POCKETS (make 2)

With 3¼ mm (UK 10/US 3) needles cast on 13 sts.

Work 2 rows in moss st as for back.

Keeping moss st correct, inc 1 st at each end of next and every foll alt row until there are 19 sts, taking inc sts into moss st.

Cont straight until pocket meas 5 [6, 7] cm (2 [2¼, 2¾] in) from cast-on edge, ending with a WS row.

Change to 3 mm (UK 11/US 2/3) needles.

Knit 2 rows.

Cast off.

POCKET EDGING

With RS facing and 3 mm (UK 11/US 2/3) needles, starting and ending at cast-off edge, pick up and k 40 [44, 48] sts evenly along entire side and lower edges of pocket.

Knit 1 row.

Cast off.

CABLE EDGING

Join shoulder seams. Matching centre of cast-off edge of sleeves to shoulders, sew sleeves to back and fronts. Join side and sleeve seams. Mark positions for 2 buttonholes along right front opening edge – first to be level with last inc of shaped edge and second to be level with start of front slope shaping.

With 3¼ mm (UK 10/US 3) needles cast on 8 sts.

1st row (RS): K8.

2nd and every foll alt row: K2, p4, k2.

3rd row: K2, slip next 2 sts onto cable needle and leave at front of work, k2, then k2 from cable needle, k2.

5th row: As 1st row.

6th row: As 2nd row.

These 6 rows form patt.

Cont in patt as now set until edging fits around entire hem, front opening and neck edge of cardigan, sewing in place as you go along, starting at ending at base of left side seam and with the addition of 2 buttonholes worked at positions marked as follows:

Buttonhole row (RS): K2, k2tog, (yfwd) twice, sl 1, k1, psso, k2.

Next row: K2, p1, p into front and back of double yfwd of previous row, p1, k2.

When edging is complete, cast off.

TO MAKE UP

Join cast-on and cast-off ends of edging. Sew on pockets as in photograph below. Sew on buttons.

NAUTICAL JACKET AND SOCKS

YOUR TODDLER WILL LOOK SMART IN THIS SAILOR JACKET TEAMED
WITH MATCHING SOCKS.

MATERIALS

1 x 50 g ball of Rowan 4 ply Cotton in A (red)
2 x 50 g balls of same yarn in B (white)
3 x 50 g balls of same yarn in C (blue)
Pair each of 2¾ mm (UK 12/US 2) and 3 mm (UK 11/US 2/3)
knitting needles
Set each of 4 double-pointed 2¾ mm (UK 12/US 2) and
3 mm (UK 11/US 2/3) knitting needles
4 buttons for jacket

MEASUREMENTS

To fit age	6–12	18–24 months
Actual measurement	66	73 cm
	26	28¾ in
Length	26	32 cm
	10¼	12½ in
Sleeve seam	16	19 cm
	6¼	7½ in

ABBREVIATIONS

See page 20.

TENSION

28 sts and 38 rows to 10 cm (4 in) measured over st st using
3 mm (UK 11/US 2/3) needles.

JACKET

BACK

With 2¾ mm (UK 12/US 2) needles and A, cast on 92 [102] sts.
Knit 4 rows.
Change to 3 mm (UK 11/US 2/3) needles.
Join in B and, twisting yarns together where they meet to avoid holes forming, proceed as follows:

1st row (RS): Using A k3, using B k to last 3 sts, using A k3.
2nd row: Using A k3, using B p to last 3 sts, using A k3.
Join in C.
3rd row: Using A k3, using C k to last 3 sts, using A k3.

4th row: Using A k3, using C p to last 3 sts, using A k3.
5th to 12th rows: As 1st to 4th rows, twice.
Break off A.
13th row (RS): Using B knit.
14th row: Using B purl.
15th row: Using C knit.
16th row: Using C purl.
13th to 16th rows form patt.
Cont in patt until back meas 26 [32] cm (10¼ [12½] in) from cast-on edge, ending with a WS row.
Shape shoulders
Cast off 16 [18] sts at beg of next 4 rows.

Cast off rem 28 [30] sts.

POCKET LININGS (make 2)
With 3 mm (UK 11/US 2/3) needles and B, cast on 22 sts.
Beg with 13th row, work 22 rows in patt as for back, ending with a WS row.
Break yarns and leave sts on a st holder.

LEFT FRONT
With 2¾ mm (UK 12/US 2) needles and A, cast on 46 [51] sts.
Knit 4 rows.
Change to 3 mm (UK 11/US 2/3) needles.
Join in B and, twisting yarns together where they meet to avoid holes forming, proceed as follows:
1st row (RS): Using A k3, using B k to end.
2nd row: Using B p to last 3 sts, using A k3.
Join in C.
3rd row: Using A k3, using C k to end.
4th row: Using C p to last 3 sts, using A k3.
5th to 12th rows: As 1st to 4th rows, twice.
Break off A.
Beg with 13th row, work in patt as for back for 22 rows, thus ending with a WS row.
Place pocket
Next row (RS): Using C k12 [17], slip next 22 sts onto a st holder and, in their place, k 22 sts of first pocket lining, k12.
Cont in patt until left front meas 13 [16] cm (5 [6¼] in) from cast-on edge, ending with a WS row.
Shape front slope
Place marker at beg of last row to denote start of front slope shaping.
Keeping patt correct, dec 1 st at marked edge of next and every 3rd row until 32 [36] sts rem.
Work straight until left front matches back to start of front slope shaping, ending with a WS row.

Shape shoulder
Cast off 16 [18] sts at beg of next row.
Work 1 row.
Cast off rem 16 [18] sts.

RIGHT FRONT
With 2¾ mm (UK 12/US 2) needles and A, cast on 46 [51] sts.
Knit 4 rows.
Change to 3 mm (UK 11/US 2/3) needles.
Join in B and, twisting yarns together where they meet to avoid holes forming, proceed as follows:
1st row (RS): Using B k to last 3 sts, using A k3.
2nd row: Using A k3, using B p to end.
Join in C.
3rd row: Using C k to last 3 sts, using A k3.
4th row: Using A k3, using C p to end.
5th to 12th rows: As 1st to 4th rows, twice.
Break off A.
Beg with 13th row, work in patt as for back for 22 rows, thus ending with a WS row.
Place pocket
Next row (RS): Using C k12, slip next 22 sts onto a st holder and, in their place, k 22 sts of second pocket lining, k12 [17].
Complete to match left front, reversing all shaping.

SLEEVES
With 2¾ mm (UK 12/US 2) needles and A, cast on 45 [49] sts.
Knit 4 rows.
Change to 3 mm (UK 11/US 2/3) needles.
Break off A and join in B and C.
Beg with 13th row, work in stripe patt as for back, inc 1 st at each end of next and every 3rd row until there are 81 [85] sts.
Work straight until sleeve meas 16 [19] cm (6¼ [7½] in) from cast-on edge, ending with a WS row.
Cast off.

COLLAR

With 2¾ mm (UK 12/US 2) needles and B, cast on 56 [60] sts.
Work in garter st for 10 [11] cm (4 [4¼] in), ending with a WS row.
Next row (RS): K14 [15] and turn, leaving rem sts on a holder.
Dec 1 st at end of 6th row and at same edge of every foll 4th row until 1 st rem.
Fasten off.
Return to sts left on holder and rejoin yarn with RS facing. Cast off 28 [30] sts at beg of next row. 14 [15] sts. Complete second side to match first.

COLLAR EDGING

With 2¾ mm (UK 12/US 2) needles, A and RS facing, starting and ending at fasten off points, pick up and knit 42 [45] sts along first straight row end edge, 56 [60] sts across cast-on edge, and 42 [45] sts along second straight row end edge. 140 [150] sts.
Knit 4 rows.
Cast off knitwise.

BUTTONHOLE BORDER

With 2¾ mm (UK 12/US 2) needles, A and RS facing, pick up and knit 48 [54] sts evenly along one front opening edge (right front for a girl, or left front for a boy), between cast-on edge and marker.
1st row (WS): Knit.
2nd row: K2, (cast off 2 sts, k until there are 12 [14] sts on right needle after cast-off) 3 times, cast off 2 sts, k to end.
3rd row: Knit to end, casting on 2 sts over those cast off on previous row.
4th row: Knit.
Cast off knitwise.

BUTTON BORDER

Work as for buttonhole border, picking up sts along other front opening edge and omitting buttonholes.

POCKET TOPS

Slip 22 sts of pocket opening onto 2¾ mm (UK 12/US 2) needles and rejoin A with RS facing.
Knit 3 rows.
Cast off knitwise.

TO MAKE UP

Join shoulder seams. Sew collar to back neck and front slope edges, matching back neck cast-off edges and ends of collar edging to top of borders. Matching centre of cast-off edge of sleeves to shoulders, sew sleeves to back and fronts. Join side and sleeve seams, leaving side seams open for first 16 rows. Sew pocket linings in place on inside and neatly sew down ends of pocket tops. Sew on buttons.

SOCKS (make 2)

With set of four double-pointed 2¾ mm (UK 12/US 2) needles and A, cast on 30 [36] sts evenly distributed over 3 needles.
Working in rounds throughout, proceed as follows:
1st round: Knit.
2nd round: Purl.
3rd and 4th rounds: As 1st and 2nd rounds.
Change to set of four double-pointed 3 mm (UK 11/US 2/3) needles.
Break off A and join in B and C.
5th and 6th rounds: Using B knit.
7th and 8th rounds: Using C knit.

5th to 8th rounds form patt.
Cont in patt until sock meas 9 [10] cm (3½ [4] in) from cast-on edge.
Divide for heel
Next round: K9 [11], turn and p these 9 [11] sts, then using same needle p 9 [11] sts from next needle, turn. 18 [22] sts.
Working backwards and forwards in rows, not rounds, and keeping patt correct (by changing colour at centre of row) work 8 rows in st st on these 18 [22] sts.
Turn heel
1st row (RS): K11 [13], sl 1, k1, psso, turn.
2nd row: P5, p2tog, turn.
3rd row: K5, sl 1, k1, psso, turn.
Rep last 2 rows until 9 sts rem from original 18 [22] sts.
Next row: P5, p2tog, p1. 8 sts.
Next row: K8, pick up and knit 8 [9] sts along side edge of heel, with 2nd needle k across 12 [14] sts of instep, using 3rd needle, pick up and knit 8 [9] sts along second side of heel, then k 4 sts from 1st needle. 36 [40] sts.
Mark beg of round.
Shape instep
Now working in rounds, not rows, and keeping patt correct, proceed as follows:
1st round: Knit.
2nd round: K to last 3 sts on first needle, k2tog, k1, k sts on 2nd needle, then on 3rd needle, k1, k2tog tbl, k to end.
Rep last 2 rounds until 24 [28] sts rem.
Cont without shaping until work meas 6 [7.5] cm (2½ [3] in) from marker.
Shape toe
1st round: K to last 2 sts on first needle, k2tog, on 2nd needle k2tog tbl, k to last 2 sts, k2tog, then on 3rd needle, k2tog tbl, k to end.
2nd round: Knit.
Rep last 2 rounds twice more, then 1st round 1 [2] times more. 8 sts.
Slip sts on 1st needle onto 3rd needle and then graft the two sets of 4 sts together (or turn to wrong side and cast off together) to form toe seam.

SCANDINAVIAN JACKET AND HAT

THIS JACKET WITH MATCHING HAT IS BASED ON
TRADITIONAL SCANDINAVIAN MOTIFS. FOR INDIVIDUALITY,
THE TRIMS ARE WORKED IN TWO-COLOUR GARTER STITCH.

MATERIALS

4 x 50 g balls of Rowan Designer DK in MC (navy)
2 x 50 g balls of same yarn in A (cream)
1 x 50 g ball of same yarn in B (red)
Pair each of 3¼ mm (UK 10/US 3) and 4 mm (UK 8/US 6)
knitting needles
5 buttons

MEASUREMENTS

To fit age	9–12 months
Actual measurement	70 cm
	27½ in
Length	31 cm
	12 in
Sleeve seam	22 cm
	8¾ in

ABBREVIATIONS

See page 20.

TENSION

24 sts and 28 rows to l0 cm (4 in) measured over st st using
4 mm (UK 8/US 6) needles.

NOTE

When working patt from chart, read chart from right to
left on RS k rows and from left to right on WS p rows. Use
separate lengths of yarn for each motif, twisting yarns
together where they meet to avoid holes forming. For
broken horizontal lines in B, strand yarn not in use loosely
across WS of work to keep fabric elastic.

JACKET

BACK

With 3¼ mm (UK 10/US 3) needles and MC, cast on 83 sts.
Knit 2 rows using MC.
Join in yarn A and knit 2 rows using A.
These 4 rows form striped g st patt.
Work a further 4 rows in striped g st patt.
Change to 4 mm (UK 8/US 6) needles.
Beg with a k row and starting and ending rows as indicated, work in
st st following body chart until chart row 80 has been worked, thus

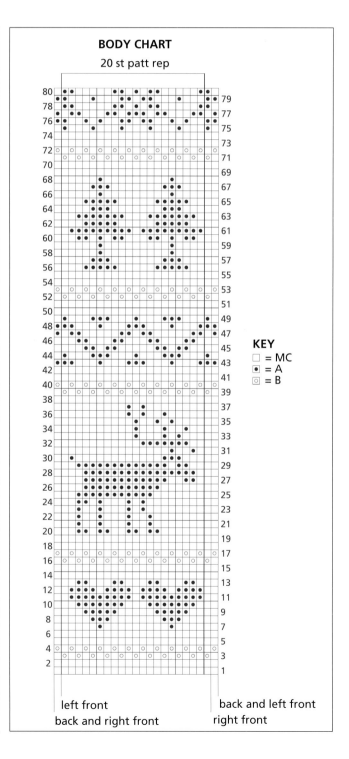

BODY CHART

20 st patt rep

KEY
☐ = MC
⊡ = A
▣ = B

left front
back and right front

back and left front
right front

ending with a WS row.

Shape shoulders

Next row (RS): Cast off 24 sts, k until there are 37 sts on right needle, cast off rem 24 sts.

Leave rem 37 sts on a holder for back neck.

LEFT FRONT

With 3¼ mm (UK 10/US 3) needles and MC, cast on 47 sts.

Work 7 rows in striped g st patt as for back.

8th row (WS): Using A, k5 and slip these 5 sts onto a safety pin for front band, k to end. 42 sts.

Change to 4 mm (UK 8/US 6) needles.

Beg with a k row and starting and ending rows as indicated, work in st st following body chart on page 92 as follows:

Cont straight until chart row 65 has been worked, thus ending with a RS row.

Shape neck

Keeping patt correct, cast off 6 sts at beg of next row and 5 sts at beg of foll alt row. 31 sts.

Dec 1 st at neck edge on next 7 rows. 24 sts.

Cont straight until chart row 80 has been worked, thus ending with a WS row.

Shape shoulder

Cast off rem 24 sts.

RIGHT FRONT

With 3¼ mm (UK 10/US 3) needles and MC, cast on 47 sts.

Work 4 rows in striped g st patt as for back.

5th row (RS): K2, (yfwd) twice (to make a buttonhole – drop extra loop on next row), k2tog, k to end. Work a further 2 rows in striped g st.

8th row (WS): Using A, k to last 5 sts and turn, leaving last 5 sts on a safety pin for front band. 42 sts.

Change to 4 mm (UK 8/US 6) needles. Beg with a k row and starting and ending rows as indicated, work in st st following body chart on page 92 as follows:

Cont straight until chart row 66 has been worked, thus ending with a WS row.

Shape neck

Keeping patt correct, cast off 6 sts at beg of next row and 5 sts at beg of foll alt row. 31 sts.

SLEEVE CHART

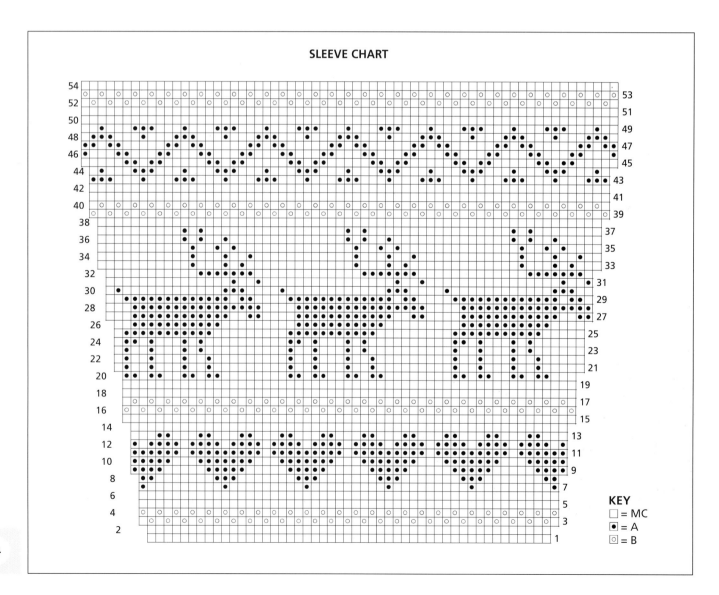

KEY
☐ = MC
⊡ = A
⊙ = B

Dec 1 st at neck edge on next 7 rows. 24 sts.
Cont straight until chart row 80 has been worked, thus ending with
a WS row.
Shape shoulder
Cast off rem 24 sts.

SLEEVES
With 3¼ mm (UK 10/US 3) needles and MC, cast on 45 sts.
Work 8 rows in striped g st patt as for back, inc 4 sts evenly across
last row. 49 sts.
Change to 4 mm (UK 8/US 6) needles.
Beg with a k row and starting and ending rows as indicated, work in
st st following sleeve chart on page 94 as follows:
Inc 1 st at each end of 3rd and every foll 6th row until there are
65 sts, working inc sts into patt.
Cont straight until chart row 54 has been worked, thus ending with
a WS row.
Cast off.

BUTTON BORDER
Join shoulder seams.
Slip 5 sts left on left front safety pin onto 3¼ mm (UK 10/US 3)
needles and rejoin yarn with RS facing.
Cont in striped g st patt as set until border, when slightly stretched,
fits up front opening edge to neck shaping, sewing in place as you
go along and ending with a RS row.
Cast off knitways (on WS).
Mark positions for 5 buttons on this border – first one level with
buttonhole already made in right front, last one 1 cm (⅜ in) down
from neck shaping and rem 3 evenly spaced between.

BUTTONHOLE BORDER
Work to match button border, rejoin yarn to sts from right front
safety pin with WS facing and with the addition of a further 4
buttonholes to correspond with positions marked for buttons
worked as follows:
Buttonhole row (RS): K2, (yfwd) twice (to make a buttonhole – drop
extra loop on next row), k2tog, k1.

COLLAR
With 3¼ mm (UK 10/US 3) needles and MC, cast on 86 sts.
Work in striped g st patt as for back until collar meas 5 cm (2 in)
from cast-on edge.
Cast off.

TO MAKE UP
Positioning ends of collar midway across top of borders, sew cast-off
edge of collar to neck edge. Matching centre of cast-off edge of
sleeves to shoulders, sew sleeves to back and fronts. Join side and
sleeve seams. Sew on buttons.

HAT

With 3¼ mm (UK 10/US 3) needles and MC, cast on 89 sts.
Work 8 rows in striped g st patt as for back of jacket.
Change to 4 mm (UK 8/US 6) needles.
Beg with a k row and starting and ending rows as indicated, work in
st st following hat chart right until chart row 40 has been worked,
thus ending with a WS row.
Break off A and B and cont in st st using MC only.
Work 4 rows.

Shape top
1st row (RS): K1, (k2tog, k6)
11 times. 78 sts.
Work 1 row.
3rd row (RS): K1, (k2tog, k5)
11 times. 67 sts.
Work 1 row.
5th row (RS): K1, (k2tog,
k4) 11 times. 56 sts.
Work 1 row.
7th row (RS): K1, (k2tog,
k3) 11 times. 45 sts.
Work 1 row.
9th row (RS): K1,
(k2tog, k2)
11 times. 34 sts.
Work 1 row.
11th row (RS): K1, (k2tog, k1) 11 times. 23 sts.
Work 1 row.
13th row (RS): K1, (k2tog) 11 times.
Break yarn and thread through rem 12 sts. Pull up tight and fasten
off securely. Join back seam. Using B, make a pompom and attach
to top of hat.

HAT CHART

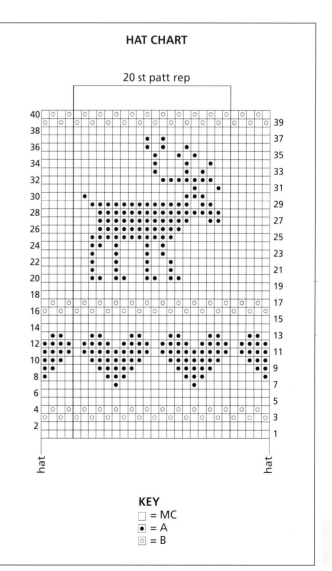

20 st patt rep

hat · · · hat

KEY
□ = MC
▣ = A
◉ = B

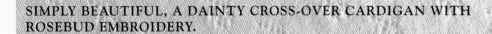

WRAP-OVER TOP

SIMPLY BEAUTIFUL, A DAINTY CROSS-OVER CARDIGAN WITH
ROSEBUD EMBROIDERY.

MATERIALS

4 [5] x 50 g balls of Rowan Cotton Glace in pale blue
Pair each of 2¾ mm (UK 12/US 2) and 3¼ mm (UK 10/US 3)
knitting needles
Oddments of same yarn in green, deep pink and blue for
embroidery

MEASUREMENTS

To fit age	0–6	6–12 months
Actual measurement	54	61 cm
	21¼	24 in
Length	21	24 cm
	8¼	9½ in
Sleeve seam	14	19 cm
	5½	7½ in

ABBREVIATIONS

See page 20.

TENSION

25 sts and 34 rows to l0 cm (4 in) measured over st st using
3¼ mm (UK 10/US 3) needles.

BACK

With 2¾ mm (UK 12/US 2) needles cast on 68 [76] sts.

1st row (RS): (K1, p1) to end.

2nd row: (P1, k1) to end.

These 2 rows form moss st.

Work a further 4 rows in moss st.

Change to 3¼ mm (UK 10/US 3) needles and, beg with a k row, work in st st until back meas 21 [24] cm (8¼ [9½] in) from cast-on edge, ending with a WS row.

Shape shoulders

Cast off 9 [10] sts at beg of next 4 rows.

Cast off rem 32 [36] sts.

LEFT FRONT

With 2¾ mm (UK 12/US 2) needles cast on 64 [74] sts.

Work 8 rows in moss st as for back, ending with a WS row.

Change to 3¼ mm (UK 10/US 3) needles.

1st row (RS): K to last 5 sts, moss st 5.

2nd row: Moss st 5, p to end.

Rep last 2 rows 4 [5] times more and then the first row again, ending with a RS row.

Shape front slope

**Next row: Moss st 1, wrap next st (by slipping next st onto right needle, taking yarn to opposite side of work between needles and then slipping same st back onto left needle), turn, moss st 1.

Next row: Moss st 2, wrap next st and turn, moss st 2.
Next row: Moss st 3, wrap next st and turn, moss st 3.
Next row: Moss st 4, wrap next st and turn, moss st 4.
Next row: Moss st 3, wrap next st and turn, moss st 3.
Next row: Moss st 2, wrap next st and turn, moss st 2.
Next row: Moss st 1, wrap next st and turn, moss st 1.**
Next row: Moss st 5 and slip these 5 sts onto a safety pin for front border, p to end. 59 [69] sts.
Next row (RS): K to last 3 sts, k2tog, k1.
Next row: P1, p2tog, p to end.
Working all decreases as set by last 2 rows, dec 1 st at front slope edge on every row until 18 [20] sts rem.
Work straight until front matches back to start of shoulder shaping, ending at side edge.
Shape shoulder
Cast off 9 [10] sts at beg of next row.
Work 1 row.
Cast off rem 9 [10] sts.

RIGHT FRONT
With 2¾ mm (UK 12/US 2) needles cast on 64 [74] sts.
Work 8 rows in moss st as for back, ending with a WS row.
Change to 3¼ mm (UK 10/US 3) needles.
1st row (RS): Moss st 5, k to end.
2nd row: P to last 5 sts, moss st 5.
Rep last 2 rows 5 [6] times more, ending with a WS row.
Shape front slope
Work as for left front from ** to **.
Next row (RS): Moss st 5, sl 1, k1, psso, k to end.
Next row: P to last 8 sts, p2tog tbl, p1 and turn, leaving last 5 sts on a safety pin for front border. 57 [67] sts.
Complete to match left front.

SLEEVES
With 2¾ mm (UK 12/US 2) needles cast on 38 [42] sts.
Work 8 rows in moss st as for back, ending with a WS row.
Change to 3¼ mm (UK 10/US 3) needles and, beg with a k row, work in st st, inc 1 st at each end of 3rd and every foll alt [3rd] row until there are 66 [70] sts.
Work straight until sleeve meas 14 [19] cm (5½ [7½] in), from cast-on edge, ending with a WS row.
Cast off.

FRONT BORDERS
Join shoulder seams.
Slip 5 sts left on safety pin onto 2¾ mm (UK 12/US 2) needles and rejoin yarn (with RS facing for left front or WS facing for right front). Cont in moss st until border, when slightly stretched, fits up front slope and across to centre back neck, sewing in place as you go along and ending with a WS row.
Cast off.
Join centre back neck seam of borders.

TIES (make 2)
With 2¾ mm (UK 12/US 2) needles cast on 5 sts.
1st row: K1, (p1, k1) twice.
Rep this row until tie meas 34 [38] cm (13½ [15] in).
Cast off.

TO MAKE UP

Attach one end of each tie to each front edge just below start of front slope shaping. Matching centre of cast-off edge of sleeves to shoulder seams, sew sleeves to back and fronts. Join side and sleeve seams, leaving an opening in right side seam for left front tie. Embroider flowers around neck edge of fronts and back as in photograph (see pages 18 to 19 for stitch details). For embroidery, split yarn into its separate strands and work using 3 strands only. For each flower, work 3 bullion stitches using deep pink, arranging them to form a triangle and wrapping yarn 8 times round needle for each stitch. In the centre, work a French knot using blue, wrapping yarn 4 times round needle. Embroider leaves next to flowers by working two lazy daisy stitches using green.

HEART, STAR AND MOON BLANKET

BABY WILL LOVE SETTLING DOWN TO SLEEP WITH THIS CHEERFUL PATCHWORK BLANKET.

STRIPE PANEL (23 sts)
1st row (RS): Using C knit.
2nd row: Using C purl.
3rd row: Using D knit.
4th row: Using D purl.
5th row: Using B knit.
6th row: Using B purl.
7th row: Using E knit.
8th row: Using E purl.
9th row: Using A knit.
10th row: Using A purl.
11th to 30th rows: As 1st to 10th rows, twice.
31st and 32nd rows: As 1st and 2nd rows.
These 32 rows complete stripe panel.

BLANKET
With 4 mm (UK 8/US 6) needles and A, cast on 145 sts.
1st row (RS): K1, (p1, k1) to end.
This row forms moss st.
Work a further 5 rows in moss st.
Keeping moss st correct (and always working moss st using A), now place panels as follows following charts on page 103.
7th row: Moss st 5, work next 23 sts as 1st row of star panel, moss st 5, work next 23 sts as 1st row of stripe panel, moss st 5, work next 23 sts as 1st row of moon panel, moss st 5, work next 23 sts as 1st row of stripe panel, moss st 5, work next 23 sts as 1st row of heart panel, moss st 5.
Cont as now set until all 32 rows of panels have been worked.
39th row: Moss st 5, (using A k23, moss st 5) 5 times.
Work 5 rows in moss st.
45th row: Moss st 5, work next 23 sts as 1st row of stripe panel, moss st 5, work next 23 sts as 1st row of star panel, moss st 5, work next 23 sts as 1st row of stripe panel, moss st 5, work next 23 sts as 1st row of moon panel, moss st 5, work next 23 sts as 1st row of stripe panel, moss st 5.
Cont as now set until all 32 rows of panels have been worked.
77th row: As 39th row.
Work 5 rows in moss st.
83rd row: Moss st 5, work next 23 sts as 1st row of heart panel, moss st 5, work next 23 sts as 1st row of stripe panel, moss st 5, work next 23 sts as 1st row of star panel, moss st 5, work next 23 sts as 1st row of stripe panel, moss st 5, work next 23 sts as 1st row of moon panel, moss st 5.
Cont as now set until all 32 rows of panels have been worked.
115th row: As 39th row.
Work 5 rows in moss st.
121st row: Moss st 5, work next 23 sts as 1st row of stripe panel, moss st 5, work next 23 sts as 1st row of heart panel, moss st 5,

MATERIALS

5 x 50 g balls of Rowan Handknit DK Cotton in A (navy)
4 x 50 g balls of same yarn in B (royal blue)
2 x 50 g balls of same yarn in each of C (deep pink),
D (yellow), and E (lime green)
Pair of 4 mm (UK 8/US 6) knitting needles

MEASUREMENTS
Completed blanket is 73 cm (28¾ in) wide and
91 cm (35¾ in) long.

ABBREVIATIONS
See page 20.

TENSION
20 sts and 30 rows to l0 cm (4 in) measured over pattern using 4 mm (UK 8/US 6) needles.

NOTE
When working panels from charts, read chart from right to left on RS k rows and from left to right on WS p rows. Use separate lengths of yarn for each block of colour, twisting yarns together where they meet to avoid holes forming.

work next 23 sts as 1st row of stripe panel, moss st 5, work next 23 sts as 1st row of star panel, moss st 5, work next 23 sts as 1st row of stripe panel, moss st 5.

Cont as now set until all 32 rows of panels have been worked.

153rd row: As 39th row.

Work 5 rows in moss st.

159th row: Moss st 5, work next 23 sts as 1st row of moon panel, moss st 5, work next 23 sts as 1st row of stripe panel, moss st 5, work next 23 sts as 1st row of heart panel, moss st 5, work next 23 sts as 1st row of stripe panel, moss st 5, work next 23 sts as 1st row of star panel, moss st 5.

Cont as now set until all 32 rows of panels have been worked.

191st row: As 39th row.

Work 5 rows in moss st.

197th row: Moss st 5, work next 23 sts as 1st row of stripe panel,

moss st 5, work next 23 sts as 1st row of moon panel, moss st 5, work next 23 sts as 1st row of stripe panel, moss st 5, work next 23 sts as 1st row of heart panel, moss st 5, work next 23 sts as 1st row of stripe panel, moss st 5.

Cont as now set until all 32 rows of panels have been worked.

229th row: As 39th row.

Work 5 rows in moss st.

235th row: As 7th row.

Cont as now set until all 32 rows of panels have been worked.

267th row: As 39th row.

Work 5 rows in moss st.

Cast off in moss st.

Using same colours as for motifs, embroider stars onto heart, moon and star panels as on charts right. For each star, work 3 straight stitches that cross at centre.

HEART PANEL

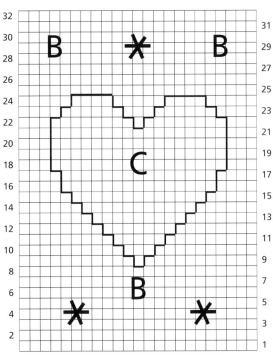

MOON PANEL

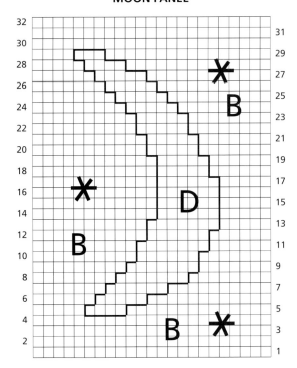

STAR PANEL

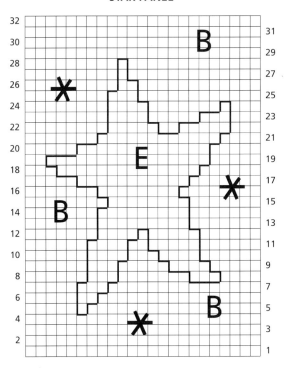

LACY SHAWL

MAKE THIS A FAMILY HEIRLOOM. A SPECIAL SHAWL TO WRAP YOUR NEWBORN IN.

MATERIALS

11 x 50 g balls of Jaeger Matchmaker Merino 4 ply in cream
Pair of 3¼ mm (UK 10/US 3) knitting needles

MEASUREMENTS
Completed shawl is 108 cm (42½ in) wide and 114 cm (44¾ in) long.

ABBREVIATIONS
See page 20.

TENSION
28 sts and 36 rows to 10 cm (4 in) measured over lace patt using 3¼ mm (UK 10/US 3) needles.

MAIN SECTION

With 3¼ mm (UK 10/US 3) needles cast on 279 sts.

Work in lace patt as follows:

1st row (RS): Knit.

2nd and every alt row: Purl.

3rd row: K2, (yfwd, sl 1, k1, psso, k16) to last 7 sts, yfwd, sl 1, k1, psso, k5.

5th row: K3, (yfwd, sl 1, k1, psso, k16) to last 6 sts, yfwd, sl 1, k1, psso, k4.

7th row: K4, (yfwd, sl 1, k1, psso, k16) to last 5 sts, yfwd, sl 1, k1, psso, k3.

9th row: K2, (k2tog, yfwd, k1, yfwd, sl 1, k1, psso, k13) to last 7 sts, k2tog, yfwd, k1, yfwd, sl 1, k1, psso, k2.

11th row: K1, (k2tog, yfwd, k3, yfwd, sl 1, k1, psso, k11) to last 8 sts, k2tog, yfwd, k3, yfwd, sl 1, k1, psso, k1.

13th row: As 7th row.

15th row: As 9th row.

17th row: K3, (yfwd, sl 1, k2tog, psso, yfwd, k15) to last 6 sts, yfwd, sl 1, k2tog, psso, yfwd, k3.

19th and 21st rows: Knit.

23rd row: K11, (yfwd, sl 1, k1, psso, k16) to last 16 sts, yfwd, sl 1, k1, psso, k14.

25th row: K12, (yfwd, sl 1, k1, psso, k16) to last 15 sts, yfwd, sl 1, k1, psso, k13.

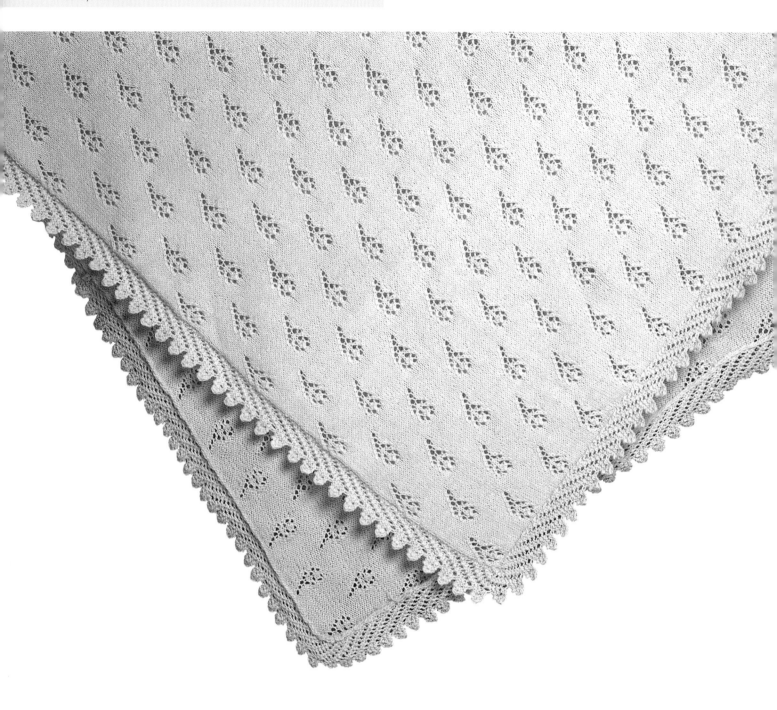

27th row: K13, (yfwd, sl 1, k1, psso, k16) to last 14 sts, yfwd, sl 1, k1, psso, k12.

29th row: K11, (k2tog, yfwd, k1, yfwd, sl 1, k1, psso, k13) to last 16 sts, k2tog, yfwd, k1, yfwd, sl 1, k1, psso, k11.

31st row: K10, (k2tog, yfwd, k3, yfwd, sl 1, k1, psso, k11) to last 17 sts, k2tog, yfwd, k3, yfwd, sl 1, k1, psso, k10.

33rd row: As 27th row.

35th row: As 29th row.

37th row: K12, (yfwd, sl 1, k2tog, psso, yfwd, k15) to last 15 sts, yfwd, sl 1, k2tog, psso, yfwd, k12.

39th row: Knit.

40th row: Purl.

These 40 rows form patt.

Cont in patt until work meas 106 cm (41¾ in) from cast-on edge, ending with a 20th patt row.

Cast off.

EDGING

With 3¼ mm (UK 10/US 3) needles cast on 8 sts.

1st row (RS): K6, inc in next st, bring yarn to front of work, sl 1 purlwise.

2nd row: K1 tbl, k1, (yfwd, sl 1, k1, psso, k1) twice, bring yarn to front of work, sl 1 purlwise. 9 sts.

Now work in patt as follows:

1st row (RS): K1 tbl, k7, inc in last st, turn and cast on 2 sts. 12 sts.

2nd row: K1, inc in next st, k2, (yfwd, sl 1, k1, psso, k1) twice, yfwd, k1, bring yarn to front of work, sl 1 purlwise. 14 sts.

3rd row: K1 tbl, k11, inc in next st, bring yarn to front of work, sl 1 purlwise. 15 sts.

4th row: K1 tbl, inc in next st, k2, (yfwd, sl 1, k1, psso, k1) 3 times, k1, bring yarn to front of work, sl 1 purlwise. 16 sts.

5th row: K1 tbl, k13, k2tog. 15 sts.

6th row: Sl 1 purlwise, take yarn to back of work, k1, psso, sl 1, k1, psso, k4, (yfwd, sl 1, k1, psso, k1) twice, bring yarn to front of work, sl 1 purlwise. 13 sts.

7th row: K1 tbl, k10, k2tog. 12 sts.

8th row: Cast off 3 sts (1 st on right needle), k2, yfwd, sl 1, k1, psso, k1, yfwd, sl 1, k1, psso, bring yarn to front of work, sl 1 purlwise. 9 sts.

Last 8 rows form patt.

Cont in patt as now set until edging fits around entire outer edge of main section, ending with 8th patt row.

Cast off.

TO MAKE UP

Join cast-on and cast-off ends of edging. Sew edging to main section, easing edging around corners.

TOY DOG

WHO COULD RESIST PATCH? THIS CUDDLY DOG DESERVES
A GOOD HOME.

MATERIALS

2 x 50 g balls of Jaeger Persia in A (beige)
1 x 50 g ball of same yarn in B (cream)
Oddment of DK yarn in C (brown)
Pair of 3¾ mm (UK 9/US 5) knitting needles
Washable toy filling

MEASUREMENTS
Completed dog is approximately 18 cm (7 in) tall and
31 cm (12 in) long.

ABBREVIATIONS
See page 20.

TENSION
20 sts and 32 rows to 10 cm (4 in) measured over rev st st
using 3¾ mm (UK 9/US 5) needles.

FIRST SIDE OF BODY
Back leg
**With A, cast on 18 sts.
Beg with a p row, cont in rev st st as follows:
Work 2 rows.
3rd row (RS): P1, (p2tog) 3 times, (p1, p2tog) twice, p5. 13 sts.
Work 5 rows.
Inc 1 st at beg of next row. 14 sts.
Work 1 row.
Next row (RS): Inc in first st, p to last 2 sts, p2tog. 14 sts.
Work 1 row.
Rep last 2 rows once more.
Inc 1 st at beg of next row. 15 sts.
Work 3 rows.
Inc 1 st at each end of next and foll 4th row. 19 sts.**
Dec 1 st at end of next row. 18 sts.
Leave these sts on a holder.
Front leg
***With A, cast on 17 sts.
Beg with a p row, cont in rev st st as follows:
Work 2 rows.
3rd row (RS): P1, (p2tog) 3 times, p1, p2tog, p7. 13 sts.
Work 5 rows.
Next row (RS): P2tog, p to last st, inc in last st. 13 sts.
Work 3 rows.

Rep last 4 rows twice more.***
Shape side of body
Mark end of last row.
Inc 1 st at beg of next row. 14 sts.
Mark end of last row.
Next row (WS): Cast on 5 sts, k to last st, inc in last st. 20 sts.
Inc 1 st at beg of next row, then cast on 5 sts at beg of foll row. 26 sts.
Mark beg of last row.
Join legs
Next row (RS): Inc in first st, p rem 25 sts of front leg, then p across 18 sts of back leg. 45 sts.
Work 4 rows.

Mark end of last row.
Work 5 rows.
Mark end of last row.
Cast off 2 sts at beg of next row. 43 sts.
Work 5 rows.
Dec 1 st at beg of next row. 42 sts.
Work 1 row.
Mark beg of last row.
Work 2 rows.
Dec 1 st at end of next row. 41 sts.
Work 3 rows.
Next row (RS): Cast off 28 sts, p to last 2 sts, p2tog. 12 sts.

Shape tail

Dec 1 st at end of next row, and at beg of foll row. 10 sts.

Work 1 row.

Dec 1 st at each end of next row. 8 sts.

Work 1 row.

Dec 1 st at beg of next and foll alt row. 6 sts.

Work 3 rows.

Cast off.

SECOND SIDE OF BODY

Work as for first side of body, reversing shapings by reading k for p and p for k.

INNER SIDE OF BACK LEGS

First leg

Work as for back leg of first side of body from ** to **.

Work 1 row.

Cast off 7 sts at beg of next row, and 6 sts at beg of foll alt row.

Work 1 row.

Cast off rem 6 sts.

Second leg

Work as for first leg, reversing shapings by reading k for p and p for k.

INNER SIDE OF FRONT LEGS

First leg

Work as for front leg of first side of body from *** to ***.

Cast off 7 sts at beg of next row.

Work 1 row.

Cast off rem 6 sts.

Second leg

Work as for first leg, reversing shapings by reading k for p and p for k.

SOLES

Back legs (make 2)

Using two strands of A held together, cast on 4 sts.

Beg with a p row, cont in rev st st as follows:

Inc 1 st at each end of next 2 rows. 8 sts.

Work 6 rows.

Dec 1 st at each end of next and foll alt row. 4 sts.

Work 1 row.

Cast off.

Front legs (make 2)

Using two strands of A held together, cast on 3 sts.

Beg with a p row, cont in rev st st as follows:

Work 1 row.

Inc 1 st at each end of next and foll alt row. 7 sts.

Work 4 rows.

Dec 1 st at each end of next and foll alt row. 3 sts.

Work 1 row.

Cast off.

UNDERSIDE

With B, cast on 3 sts.

Beg with a p row, cont in rev st st as follows:

Work 2 rows.

Inc 1 st at each end of next and foll 4th row. 7 sts.

Work 2 rows.

Inc 1 st at each end of next row. 9 sts.

Work 2 rows.

Mark each end of last row.

Shape for back legs

Work 2 rows.

Dec 1 st at each end of next and foll alt row. 5 sts.

Work 3 rows.

Dec 1 st at each end of next row. 3 sts.

Work 13 rows.

Inc 1 st at each end of next and foll 4th row. 7 sts.

Work 1 row.

Inc 1 st at each end of next 2 rows. 11 sts.

Mark each end of last row.

Shape tummy

Work 14 rows.

Mark each end of last row.

Shape for front legs

Dec 1 st at each end of next 2 rows. 7 sts.

Work 1 row.

Dec 1 st at each end of next and foll 3rd row. 3 sts.

Work 7 rows.

Inc 1 st at each end of next and foll 3rd row. 7 sts.

Work 1 row.

Inc 1 st each end of next row. 9 sts.

Work 2 rows.

Mark each end of last row.

Shape front gusset

Work 6 rows.

Dec 1 st at each end of next and foll 6th row. 5 sts.

Work 5 rows.

Cast off.

HEAD

First side

With A, cast on 10 sts.

Beg with a p row, cont in rev st st as follows:

Work 10 rows.

Cast on 4 sts at beg of next and foll 2 alt rows. 22 sts.

Work 1 row.

Mark end of last row.

Work 2 rows.

Cast off 7 sts at beg of next and foll alt row. 8 sts.

Work 1 row.

Cast off.

Second side

Work as first side, reversing shapings by reading k for p and p for k.

Top gusset

With A, cast on 6 sts.

Beg with a p row, cont in rev st st as follows:

Work 8 rows.

Inc 1 st at each end of next and foll 8th row. 10 sts.

Work 5 rows.

Mark each end of last row.

Work 4 rows.

Inc 1 st at each end of next and foll 4th row. 14 sts.

Work 1 row.

Inc 1 st at each end of next 2 rows. 18 sts.

Work 16 rows.

Dec 1 st at each end of next 2 rows. 14 sts.

Next row (RS): (P2tog, p2) 3 times, p2tog. 10 sts.

Next row: (K2tog) twice, k2, (k2tog) twice. 6 sts.

Cast off, working centre 2 sts tog.

Underchin gusset

With A, cast on 7 sts.

Beg with a p row, cont in rev st st as follows:

Work 12 rows.

Inc 1 st at each end of next and foll 4th row. 11 sts.

Work 15 rows.

Mark each end of last row.

Work 1 row.

Dec 1 st at each end of next 3 rows. 5 sts.

Cast off.

EARS

Top layers (make 2)

With A, cast on 8 sts.

Beg with a p row, cont in rev st st as follows:

Work 8 rows.

Inc 1 st at each end of next and foll 4th row. 12 sts.

Work 13 rows.

Dec 1 st at each end of next and foll 4th row. 8 sts.

Work 1 row.

Dec 1 st at each end of next 2 rows. 4 sts.

Cast off.

Linings (make 2)

With B, work as for top layer.

NOSE

With C, cast on 5 sts.

Beg with a k row, cont in st st as follows:

Work 1 row.

Inc 1 st at each end of next 2 rows. 9 sts.

Work 7 rows.

Dec 1 st at each end of next 2 rows. 5 sts.

Work 1 row.

Cast off.

EYE PATCH

With B, cast on 5 sts.

Beg with a p row, cont in rev st st as follows:

Work 1 row.

Inc 1 st at each end of next and foll alt row. 9 sts.

Work 6 rows.

Dec 1 st at beg of next row, and at each end of foll row.

Rep last 2 rows once more. 3 sts.

Work 1 row.

Cast off.

TO MAKE UP

Join inner legs to side legs, leaving cast-on edges open and matching top edges to markers. Sew in soles. Join top seam of sides from front edge to end of top of tail, leaving ridge on right side. With C, work blanket stitch along ridge (see page 19 for stitch details). Join back seam from top of tail to first marker. Placing cast-on edge of underside to back seam, cast-off edge to markers at front edge and matching markers, sew underside in position. Join underchin gusset to sides of head from cast-on edge to markers. Sew top gusset to sides and underchin gusset, sewing row ends of gusset from cast-on edge to marker to straight edge of sides. Insert toy filling into body and head. Sew head to body. With paired ear pieces together, work blanket st around edges with C, leaving cast-on edge open. Sew cast-on edge of ears to top of head. Sew on eye patch. Run a gathering thread around edge of nose. Pull up and insert toy filling, then sew in position. With C, embroider eyes and claws.

STRIPED BAG AND HAT

EVERY LITTLE GIRL WILL LOVE THIS SET.

MATERIALS

1 x 50 g ball of Jaeger Pure Cotton in each of A (deep pink), B (blue), C (aqua), D (cream), E (light pink) and F (mid-pink)
Pair each of 2¾ mm (UK 12/US 2) and 3 mm (UK 11/US 2/3) knitting needles

MEASUREMENTS
To fit age   6–12 months

ABBREVIATIONS
See page 20.

TENSION
25 sts and 34 rows to 10 cm (4 in) measured over st st on 3 mm (UK 11/US 2/3) needles.

BAG

With 3 mm (UK 11/US 2/3) needles and A, cast on 76 sts.
Beg with a k row, work in striped st st as follows:
1st to 3rd rows: Using A.
4th and 5th rows: Using B.
6th row: Using C.
7th row: Using D.
8th and 9th rows: Using E.
10th and 11th rows: Using A.
12th and 13th rows: Using F.
14th row: Using B.
15th and 16th rows: Using A.
17th row: Using C.
18th row: Using D.
19th and 20th rows: Using B.
21st row: Using F.
22nd row: Using A.
23rd and 24th rows: Using E.
25th row: Using C.
26th and 27th rows: Using D.
28th and 29th rows: Using A.
30th to 32nd rows: Using E.
These 32 rows form stripe sequence.
Cont in stripe sequence as now set until work meas 19 cm (7½ in) from cast-on edge.
Cast off.
Join side and lower edge seam. Fold last 8 rows to inside around upper edge and slip stitch in place.
Strap
With 2¾ mm (UK 12/US 2) needles and A, cast on 4 sts.
Work in g st until strap meas 50 cm (19½ in).
Cast off.
Sew ends of strap to inside of upper edge of bag at sides. Using A, make a twisted cord about 70 cm (27½ in) long and 2 tassels.
Thread cord through casing around upper edge, bringing cord out through knitting directly below one end of strap. Attach tassels to ends of cord.

HAT

With 3 mm (UK 11/US 2/3) needles and A, cast on 109 sts.
Beg with a k row, work in st st and stripe sequence as for bag until hat meas 11 cm (4¼ in) from cast-on edge, ending with a WS row.

Shape crown

Keeping stripe sequence correct, proceed as follows:

1st row (RS): K1, (k2tog, k10) to end. 100 sts.
2nd and every foll alt row: Purl.
3rd row: K1, (k2tog, k9) to end. 91 sts.
5th row: K1, (k2tog, k8) to end. 82 sts.
7th row: K1, (k2tog, k7) to end. 73 sts.
9th row: K1, (k2tog, k6) to end. 64 sts.
11th row: K1, (k2tog, k5) to end. 55 sts.
13th row: K1, (k2tog, k4) to end. 46 sts.
15th row: K1, (k2tog, k3) to end. 37 sts.
17th row: K1, (k2tog, k2) to end. 28 sts.
19th row: K1, (k2tog, k1) to end. 19 sts.
21st row: K1, (k2tog) to end.

Break yarn and thread through rem 10 sts. Pull up tight and fasten off securely.

Brim

With 3 mm (UK 11/US 2/3) needles and A, pick up and knit 113 sts evenly along cast-on edge of first section.

Working stripe sequence *in reverse* and starting with a p row, cont in st st as follows:

Work 1 row.

2nd row (RS): K1, (m1, k8) 14 times. 127 sts.

Work 2 rows.

5th row: (P9, m1) 14 times, p1. 141 sts.

Work 2 rows.

8th row: K1, (m1, k10) 14 times. 155 sts.

Work 2 rows.

11th row: (P11, m1) 14 times, p1. 169 sts.

Work 1 row.

Cast off loosely.

Join back seam.

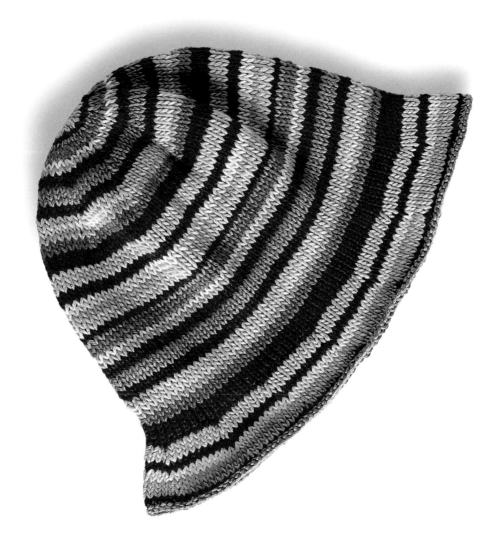

BABY BLANKET

THIS BEAUTIFULLY SIMPLE PATCHWORK BLANKET IS BASED ON SHAKER DESIGNS.

BLANKET
With 4 mm (UK 8/US 6) needles and A, cast on 111 sts. Follow charts on page 119.
1st row (RS): K1, work next 25 sts as 1st row of star panel, k3, work next 25 sts as 1st row of diamond panel, k3, work next 25 sts as 1st row of house panel, k3, work next 25 sts as 1st row of heart panel, k1.
2nd row: P1, work next 25 sts as 2nd row of heart panel, k3, work next 25 sts as 2nd row of house panel, k3, work next 25 sts as 2nd row of diamond panel, k3, work next 25 sts as 2nd row of star panel, p1.
These 2 rows set position of first band of panels with 3 sts in g st between panels and 1 st in st st at each end of rows. Keeping patt correct as now set, cont until all 36 rows of panels are complete. Work 4 rows in g st.
41st row (RS): K1, work next 25 sts as 1st row of heart panel, k3, work next 25 sts as 1st row of star panel, k3, work next 25 sts as 1st row of diamond panel, k3, work next 25 sts as 1st row of house panel, k1.

MATERIALS

8 x 50 g balls of Rowan Handknit DK Cotton in A (cream)
1 x 50 g ball of same yarn in B (pale blue)
Pair each of 3¼ mm (UK10/US 3) and 4 mm (UK 8/US 6) knitting needles

MEASUREMENTS
Completed blanket is approximately 72 cm (28¼ in) wide and 90 cm (35½ in) long.

ABBREVIATIONS
See page 20.

TENSION
22 sts and 30 rows to l0 cm (4 in) measured over pattern using 4 mm (UK 8/US 6) needles.

NOTES
When working patt from charts, read charts from right to left on RS rows and from left to right on WS rows. Use separate lengths of yarn for each motif, twisting yarns together where they meet to avoid holes forming.
Make bobble as follows: (k1, yfwd, k1) all into next st, turn, k3, turn, p3, turn, k3, turn, sl 1, k2tog, psso.

42nd row: P1, work next 25 sts as 2nd row of house panel, k3, work next 25 sts as 2nd row of diamond panel, k3, work next 25 sts as 2nd row of star panel, k3, work next 25 sts as 2nd row of heart panel, p1.

These 2 rows set position of second band of panels.

Keeping patt correct as now set, cont until all 36 rows of panels are complete.

Work 4 rows in g st.

81st row (RS): K1, work next 25 sts as 1st row of house panel, k3, work next 25 sts as 1st row of heart panel, k3, work next 25 sts as 1st row of star panel, k3, work next 25 sts as 1st row of diamond panel, k1.

82nd row: P1, work next 25 sts as 2nd row of diamond panel, k3, work next 25 sts as 2nd row of star panel, k3, work next 25 sts as 2nd row of heart panel, k3, work next 25 sts as 2nd row of house panel, p1.

These 2 rows set position of third band of panels.

Keeping patt correct as now set, cont until all 36 rows of panels are complete.

Work 4 rows in g st.

121st row (RS): K1, work next 25 sts as 1st row of diamond panel, k3, work next 25 sts as 1st row of house panel, k3, work next 25 sts as 1st row of heart panel, k3, work next 25 sts as 1st row of star panel, k1.

122nd row: P1, work next 25 sts as 2nd row of star panel, k3, work next 25 sts as 2nd row of heart panel, k3, work next 25 sts as 2nd row of house panel, k3, work next 25 sts as 2nd row of diamond panel, p1.

These 2 rows set position of fourth band of panels.

Keeping patt correct as now set, cont until all 36 rows of panels are complete.

Work 4 rows in g st.

161st row (RS): K1, work next 25 sts as 1st row of star panel, k3, work next 25 sts as 1st row of diamond panel, k3, work next 25 sts as 1st row of house panel, k3, work next 25 sts as 1st row of heart panel, k1.

162nd row: P1, work next 25 sts as 2nd row of heart panel, k3, work next 25 sts as 2nd row of house panel, k3, work next 25 sts as 2nd row of diamond panel, k3, work next 25 sts as 2nd row of star panel, p1.

These 2 rows set position of fifth band of panels.

Keeping patt correct as now set, cont until all 36 rows of panels are complete.

Cast off.

EDGING

Using 3¼ mm (UK 10/US 3) needles and A, cast on 9 sts.

1st and every foll alt row (RS): Knit.

2nd row: K3, k2tog, yfwd, k2tog, (yfwd, k1) twice. 10 sts.

4th row: K2, (k2tog, yfwd) twice, k3, yfwd, k1. 11 sts.

6th row: K1, (k2tog, yfwd) twice, k5, yfwd, k1. 12 sts.

8th row: K3, (yfwd, k2tog) twice, k1, k2tog, yfwd, k2tog. 11 sts.

10th row: K4, yfwd, k2tog, yfwd, k3tog, yfwd, k2tog. 10 sts.

12th row: K5, yfwd, k3tog, yfwd, k2tog. 9 sts.

These 12 rows form patt.

Cont in patt until edging fits around entire outer edge of blanket, ending with a 12th patt row.

Cast off.

TO MAKE UP

Join cast-on and cast-off ends of edging. Sew edging in place to outer edge of blanket, easing in fullness around corners.

STAR PANEL

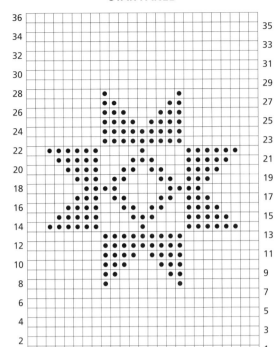

DIAMOND PANEL

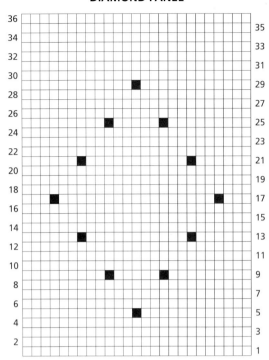

HOUSE PANEL

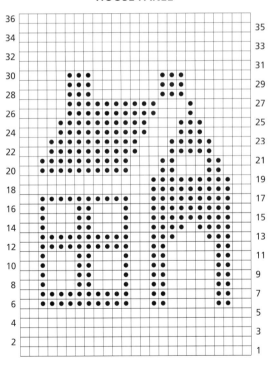

HEART PANEL

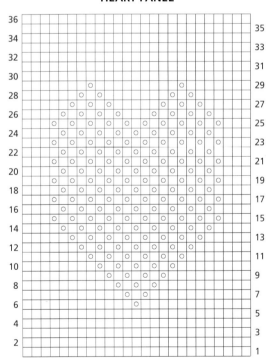

KEY

☐ = using A, k on RS rows and p on WS rows
◦ = using A, p on RS rows and k on WS rows
■ = using A, make bobble
• = using B, k on RS rows and p on WS rows

119

RABBIT FAMILY

KNIT ONE AND YOU'LL BE HOOKED. AN ADORABLE SET OF RABBITS
FOR KNITTERS WHO LIKE A CHALLENGE. KEEP GOING AND YOU'LL
SOON HAVE THE WHOLE FAMILY.

MATERIALS

Baby [Child, Adult] Rabbit
1 [2, 4] x 50 g balls of Rowan Wool Cotton in A (cream)
1 x 50 g ball of Rowan True 4 ply Botany in each of
B (beige), C (dark grey) and D (lilac for baby, blue for child,
red for mummy or green for daddy)
1 x 50 g ball of Rowan Felted Tweed in E (grey)
Oddment of black, pink and brown yarn for embroidery
Pair each of 3 mm (UK 11/US 2/3), 3¼ mm (UK 10/US 3)
and 3¾ mm (UK 9/US 5) knitting needles
White sewing thread and white nail varnish (optional)
for whiskers
Length of narrow elastic
Washable toy filling

MEASUREMENTS

Completed baby [child, adult] rabbit is approximately
14 [25, 38] cm (5½ [10, 15] in) tall.

ABBREVIATIONS

See page 20.

TENSION

Wool Cotton: 28 sts and 46 rows to
10 cm (4 in) measured over moss st
using 3 mm (UK 11/US 2/3) needles.
True 4 ply Botany: 28 sts and 36 rows
to 10 cm (4 in) measured over st st
using 3¼ mm (UK 10/US 3) needles.
Felted Tweed: 24 sts and 32 rows to
l0 cm (4 in) measured over st st
using 3¾ mm (UK 9/US 5)
needles.

BABY RABBIT

LEGS (make 4)
With 3 mm (UK 11/US 2/3) needles and A, cast on 7 sts.
1st row (RS): K1, (p1, k1) to end.
This row forms moss st.
Cont in moss st, inc 1 st at end of next row, then at beg of foll row. 9 sts.
Work 1 row.
Dec 1 st at end of next row. 8 sts.
Cast off 3 sts at beg of next row for top of foot. 5 sts.
Work 2 rows.

Inc 1 st at each end of next and foll 3rd row. 9 sts.
Work 6 rows.
Dec 1 st at each end of next and foll alt row. 5 sts.
Dec 1 st at each end of next row. 3 sts.
Work 1 row.
Cast off.

SOLES (make 2)
With 3 mm (UK 11/US 2/3) needles and B, cast on 3 sts.
Beg with a k row, work in st st throughout as follows:
Work 1 row.

Inc 1 st at each end of next row. 5 sts.
Work 5 rows.
Dec 1 st at each end of next row. 3 sts.
Work 1 row.
Cast off.

ARMS (make 4)

With 3 mm (UK 11/US 2/3) needles and A, cast on 3 sts.
Work in moss st as for legs throughout as follows:
Work 1 row.
Inc 1 st at end of next row and at same edge of foll 2 rows. 6 sts.
Work 1 row.
Inc 1 st at end of next row. 7 sts.
Work 1 row.
Dec 1 st at beg and inc 1 st at end of next row. 7 sts.
Work 1 row.
Inc 1 st at end of next row. 8 sts.
Work 1 row.
Dec 1 st at beg of next row. 7 sts.
Inc 1 st at beg of next row. 8 sts.
Work 5 rows.
Dec 1 st at each end of next and foll alt row. 4 sts.
Dec 1 st at each end of next row. 2 sts.
Work 1 row.
Cast off.

PAWS (make 2)

With 3 mm (UK 11/US 2/3) needles and B, cast on 3 sts.
Beg with a k row, work in st st throughout as follows:
Work 1 row.
Inc 1 st at each end of next row. 5 sts.
Work 3 rows.
Dec 1 st at each end of next row. 3 sts.
Work 1 row.
Cast off.

BODY (make 2)

With 3 mm (UK 11/US 2/3) needles and A, cast on 3 sts.
Work in moss st as for legs throughout as follows:
Work 1 row.
Inc 1 st at each end of next 2 rows, then on foll 2 alt rows. 11 sts.
Work 9 rows.
Dec 1 st at each end of next and foll 4th row. 7 sts.
Work 4 rows.
Cast off.

SIDE OF HEAD (make 2)

With 3 mm (UK 11/US 2/3) needles and A, cast on 3 sts.
Work in moss st as for legs throughout as follows:
Work 1 row.
Inc 1 st at each end of next row, then at end of foll row. 6 sts.

Inc 1 st at each end of next row. 8 sts.
Work 1 row.
Inc 1 st at beg of next and foll alt row. 10 sts.
Work 2 rows.
Place marker at end of last row.
Dec 1 st at beg of next and foll alt row. 8 sts.
Dec 1 st at beg of next 3 rows. 5 sts.
Dec 1 st at each end of next row. 3 sts.
Work 1 row.
Cast off.

HEAD GUSSET

With 3 mm (UK 11/US 2/3) needles and A, cast on 3 sts.
Work in moss st as for legs throughout as follows:
Work 2 rows.
Inc 1 st at each end of next and foll 4th row. 7 sts.
Work 17 rows.
Dec 1 st at each end of next and foll 3rd row. 3 sts.
Work 2 rows.
Cast off.

OUTER EARS (make 2)

With 3 mm (UK 11/US 2/3) needles and A, cast on 5 sts.
Work in moss st as for legs throughout as follows:
Work 4 rows.
Inc 1 st at each end of next and foll 4th row. 9 sts.
Work 13 rows.
Dec 1 st at each end of next and foll 2 alt rows. 3 sts.
Work 1 row.
Next row: Work 3 tog and fasten off.

INNER EARS (make 2)

With 3 mm (UK 11/US 2/3) needles and B, cast on 5 sts.
Beg with a k row, work in st st throughout as follows:
Work 4 rows.
Inc 1 st at each end of next and foll 4th row. 9 sts.
Work 13 rows.
Dec 1 st at each end of next and foll 2 alt rows. 3 sts.
Work 1 row.
Next row: Work 3 tog and fasten off.

CHILD RABBIT

LEGS (make 4)

With 3 mm (UK 11/US 2/3) needles and A, cast on 13 sts.
1st row (RS): K1, (p1, k1) to end.
This row forms moss st.
Cont in moss st, inc 1 st at end of next row and at same edge on foll row. 15 sts.
Work 4 rows.
Dec 1 st at beg of next and foll alt row. 13 sts.
Work 1 row.
Cast off 5 sts at beg of next row for top of foot. 8 sts.
Work 3 rows.
Inc 1 st at each end of next and every foll 4th row until there are 14 sts.
Work 10 rows.
Dec 1 st at each end of next and foll 2 alt rows. 8 sts.
Dec 1 st at each end of next 2 rows. 4 sts.
Work 1 row.
Cast off.

SOLES (make 2)

With 3 mm (UK 11/US 2/3) needles and two strands of B held together, cast on 2 sts.
Beg with a k row, work in st st throughout as follows:
Work 1 row.
Inc 1 st at each end of next 2 rows. 6 sts.
Work 11 rows.
Dec 1 st at each end of next and foll alt row. 2 sts.
Work 1 row.
Cast off.

ARMS (make 4)

With 3 mm (UK 11/US 2/3) needles and A, cast on 5 sts.
Work in moss st as for legs throughout as follows:
Work 1 row.
Inc 1 st at end of next row and at same edge of foll 3 rows. 9 sts.
Work 1 row.
Inc 1 st at beg of next and foll alt row. 11 sts.
*Work 1 row.
Inc 1 st at beg and dec 1 st at end of next row.
Work 1 row.
Inc 1 st at beg of next row.*
Rep from * to * once more. 13 sts.
Work 3 rows.
Inc 1 st at beg of next row. 14 sts.
Work 13 rows.
Dec 1 st at each end of next and foll 2 alt rows. 8 sts.
Dec 1 st at each end of next 2 rows. 4 sts.
Work 1 row.
Cast off.

PAWS (make 2)

With 3 mm (UK 11/US 2/3) needles and two strands of B held together, cast on 2 sts.
Beg with a k row, work in st st throughout as follows:
Work 1 row.
Inc 1 st at each end of next 2 rows. 6 sts.
Work 5 rows.
Dec 1 st at each end of next 2 rows. 2 sts.
Work 1 row.
Cast off.

BODY (make 2)

With 3 mm (UK 11/US 2/3) needles and A, cast on 9 sts.
Work in moss st as for legs throughout as follows:
Work 1 row.
Inc 1 st at each end of next 2 rows, then on foll alt row, then on foll 4th row. 17 sts.
Work 15 rows.
Dec 1 st at each end of next and foll 6th row, then on every foll 4th row. 11 sts.
Work 9 rows.
Cast off.

SIDE OF HEAD (make 2)

With 3 mm (UK 11/US 2/3) needles and A, cast on 5 sts.
Work in moss st as for legs throughout as follows:
Inc 1 st at beg of 1st row. 6 sts.
Inc 1 st at each end of next row, then at end of foll 4 rows. 12 sts.
Work 1 row.
Inc 1 st at end of next 3 rows. 15 sts.
Work 1 row.

Inc 1 st at end of next and foll alt row. 17 sts.
Work 2 rows.
Place marker at end of last row.
Work 1 row.
Dec 1 st at end of next and foll alt row. 15 sts.
Dec 1 st at end of next 2 rows. 13 sts.
Work 1 row.
Dec 1 st at end of next 4 rows. 9 sts.
Dec 1 st at each end of next row. 7 sts.
Dec 1 st at end of next row. 6 sts.
Work 1 row.
Cast off.

HEAD GUSSET

With 3 mm (UK 11/US 2/3) needles and A, cast on 3 sts.
Work in moss st as for legs throughout as follows:
Work 1 row.
Inc 1 st at each end of next and foll 4th row. 7 sts.
Work 35 rows.
Dec 1 st at each end of next and foll 6th row. 3 sts.
Work 5 rows.
Cast off.

OUTER EARS (make 2)

With 3 mm (UK 11/US 2/3) needles and A, cast on 9 sts.
Work in moss st as for legs throughout as follows:
Work 4 rows.
Inc 1 st at each end of next and every foll 4th row until there are 15 sts.
Work 27 rows.
Dec 1 st at each end of next and every foll alt row until 3 sts rem.
Work 1 row.
Next row: Work 3 tog and fasten off.

INNER EARS (make 2)

With 3 mm (UK 11/US 2/3) needles and two strands of B held together, cast on 6 sts.
Beg with a k row, work in st st throughout as follows:
Work 4 rows.
Inc 1 st at each end of next and every foll 4th row until there are 12 sts.
Work 21 rows.
Dec 1 st at each end of next and every foll alt row until 2 sts rem.
Work 1 row.
Next row: Work 2 tog and fasten off.

ADULT RABBIT

LEGS (make 4)

With 3 mm (UK 11/US 2/3) needles and A, cast on 25 sts.
1st row (RS): K1, (p1, k1) to end.
This row forms moss st.
Cont in moss st, inc 1 st at end of next row and at same edge on foll 2 rows. 28 sts.
Work 10 rows.
Dec 1 st at end of next and foll 2 alt rows. 25 sts.
Work 2 rows.
Cast off 9 sts at beg of next row for top of foot. 16 sts.
Work 8 rows.
Inc 1 st at each end of next and foll 4th row, then on every foll 6th row until there are 24 sts.

Work 11 rows.
Dec 1 st at each end of next and foll 4th row, then on every foll alt row until 16 sts rem.
Dec 1 st at each end of next 3 rows. 10 sts.
Work 1 row.
Cast off.

SOLES (make 2)

With 3 mm (UK 11/US 2/3) needles and two strands of B held together, cast on 3 sts.
Beg with a k row, work in st st throughout as follows:
Work 1 row.
Inc 1 st at each end of next 2 rows, then on foll alt row. 9 sts.
Work 19 rows.
Dec 1 st at each end of next and foll alt row, then on foll row. 3 sts.
Work 1 row.
Cast off.

ARMS (make 4)

With 3 mm (UK 11/US 2/3) needles and A, cast on 7 sts.
Work in moss st as for legs throughout as follows:
Work 1 row.
Inc 1 st at end of next row and at same edge of foll 4 rows, then on foll 5 alt rows. 17 sts.
*Dec 1 st at end of next row.
Inc 1 st at end of next and foll alt row.*
Rep from * to * once more. 19 sts.
Dec 1 st at end of next row.
Inc 1 st at end of next row. 19 sts.
Work 4 rows.
Inc 1 st at beg of next row. 20 sts.
Work 27 rows.
Dec 1 st at each end of next and foll 4th row, then on foll 2 alt rows. 12 sts.
Dec 1 st at each end of next 3 rows. 6 sts.
Work 1 row.
Cast off.

PAWS (make 2)

With 3 mm (UK 11/US 2/3) needles and two strands of B held together, cast on 4 sts.
Beg with a k row, work in st st throughout as follows:
Work 1 row.
Inc 1 st at each end of next 2 rows, then on foll alt row. 10 sts.
Work 4 rows.
Dec 1 st at each end of next and foll alt row, then on foll row. 4 sts.
Work 1 row.
Cast off.

BODY (make 2)

With 3 mm (UK 11/US 2/3) needles and A, cast on 13 sts.
Work in moss st as for legs throughout as follows:
Work 1 row.
Inc 1 st at each end of next 5 rows, then on foll 2 alt rows. 27 sts.
Inc 1 st at each end of every foll 4th row until there are 31 sts.
Work 22 rows.
Dec 1 st at each end of next and every foll 6th row until 25 sts rem, then on every foll 4th row until 21 sts rem.
Work 14 rows.
Cast off.

SIDE OF HEAD (make 2)

With 3 mm (UK 11/US 2/3) needles and A, cast on 9 sts.
Work in moss st as for legs throughout as follows:
Inc 1 st at beg of 1st row. 10 sts.
Inc 1 st at each end of next row, then at end of foll row. 13 sts.
Inc 1 st at each end of next row, then at beg of foll 3 rows. 18 sts.
Inc 1 st at each end of next row. 20 sts.
Work 1 row.
Inc 1 st at end of next row, then at beg of foll 3 rows. 24 sts.
Inc 1 st at each end of next row. 26 sts.
Work 1 row.
Inc 1 st at end of next row, then at beg of foll row. 28 sts.
Work 1 row.
Inc 1 st at beg of next row, then at end of foll row. 30 sts.
Work 1 row.
Inc 1 st at end of next row. 31 sts.
Work 2 rows.
Place marker at end of last row.
Work 2 rows.
Dec 1 st at beg of next and foll alt row. 29 sts.

Dec 1 st at end of next row. 28 sts.
Work 1 row.
Dec 1 st at end of next row, then at beg of foll row. 26 sts.
Work 1 row.
Dec 1 st at each end of next row. 24 sts.
Dec 1 st at end of next and foll alt row. 22 sts.
Dec 1 st at each end of next and foll alt row. 18 sts.
Dec 1 st at end of next 2 rows, then at each end of foll 2 rows.
12 sts.
Cast off.

HEAD GUSSET

With 3 mm (UK 11/US 2/3) needles and A, cast on 3 sts.
Work in moss st as for legs throughout as follows:
Work 2 rows.
Inc 1 st at each end of next and foll 2 alt rows, then on every foll
4th row until there are 13 sts.
Work 43 rows.
Dec 1 st at each end of next and foll 8th row, then on foll 6th row,
then on foll 4th row. 5 sts.

Work 3 rows.
Cast off.

OUTER EARS (make 2)

With 3 mm (UK 11/US 2/3) needles and A, cast on 13 sts.
Work in moss st as for legs throughout as follows:
Work 4 rows.
Inc 1 st at each end of next and every foll 4th row until there are 21 sts.
Work 47 rows.
Dec 1 st at each end of next and every foll alt row until 3 sts rem.
Work 1 row.
Next row: Work 3 tog and fasten off.

INNER EARS (make 2)

With 3 mm (UK 11/US 2/3) needles and two strands of B held together, cast on 10 sts.
Beg with a k row, work in st st throughout as follows:
Work 4 rows.
Inc 1 st at each end of next and every foll 4th row until there are 18 sts.
Work 35 rows.
Dec 1 st at each end of next and every foll alt row until 2 sts rem.
Work 1 row.
Next row: Work 2 tog and fasten off.

TO MAKE UP

Join pairs of leg and arm pieces, leaving openings. Insert toy filling and close openings. Attach soles and paws as in photograph on page 121. Join body pieces, leaving cast-off edge open. Insert toy filling and close opening.

Join head pieces from cast-on edge to marker. Sew head gusset to head pieces, placing gusset cast-off edge level with cast-on edges of sides and centre of gusset cast-on edge to front seam. Insert toy filling. Run gathering thread around open edge, pull up tightly and fasten off securely. Sew head to body.

Pin arms into position on body. Using two strands of A held together, attach arms to body by taking one long stitch right through first arm, then body, then second arm. Take another long stitch back in exactly the same way and fasten off securely. Attach legs in same way.

Join outer and inner ears, then sew cast-on edges of ears to head. Using black yarn, embroider eyes. Using pink yarn, embroider nose. Outline nose and embroider mouth using brown. Using two strands of sewing thread held together, embroider whiskers on either side of nose and stiffen them by painting with nail varnish (optional). Using A, make a small pompom and attach to form tail.

TROUSERS

LEGS (make 2)

With 3¼ mm (UK 10/US 3) needles and C, cast on 7 [12, 20] sts.
Beg with a k row, work in 4 row st st stripe sequence (of 2 rows using C and 2 rows using D) throughout as follows:
Work 1 row.
Inc 1 st at beg of next row and at same edge of foll 2 [4, 6] rows. 10 [17, 27] sts.
Work 1 row.
Cast on 7 [13, 25] sts at beg of next row. 17 [30, 52] sts.
Work 19 [31, 59] rows.
Cast off 7 [13, 25] sts at beg of next row. 10 [17, 27] sts.
Dec 1 st at end of next row and at same edge on foll 2 [4, 6] rows. 7 [12, 20] sts.
Cast off.

HEM EDGING

With 3¼ mm (UK 10/US 3) needles, RS facing and C, pick up and knit 19 [32, 54] sts along lower edge (longer row end edge) of leg.
Knit 2 rows.
Cast off knitwise.

WAIST EDGING

Join front crotch seam.
With 3¼ mm (UK 10/US 3) needles, RS facing and C, pick up and knit 28 [42, 80] sts along upper edge of both legs.
Next row: (K1, p1) to end.
Rep last row 2 [3, 4] times more.
Cast off in rib.

TO MAKE UP

Join back crotch seam, leaving an opening for tail. Join inside leg seams. Cut elastic to fit waist of rabbit and join ends. Lay elastic over inside of waist edging and secure in position by working herringbone stitch over it.

SWEATER

BACK AND FRONT (alike)

With 3¾ mm (UK 9/US 5) needles and E, cast on 16 [26, 48] sts.
1st row (RS): (K1, p1) to end.
Rep this row 1 [2, 3] times more, inc 0 [1, 1] st at centre of last row. 16 [27, 49] sts.
Beg with a k row, work in st st throughout as follows:
Work 3 [4, 6] rows.
Place markers at both ends of last row.
Work 10 [20, 33] rows, ending with a RS row.
Knit 2 rows.
Cast off knitwise.

SLEEVES

Join shoulder seams, leaving opening large enough for head.
With 3¾ mm (UK 9/US 5) needles, RS facing and E, pick up and knit 20 [32, 50] sts along side edge of body between markers.
Beg with a p row, work in st st throughout as follows:
Work 1 [3, 7] rows.
Dec 1 st at each end of next and every foll 3rd [4th, 4th] row until 16 [26, 42] sts rem.
Work 1 row.
Work 2 [3, 4] rows in rib as for back and front.
Cast off in rib.

TO MAKE UP

Join side and sleeve seams.

SUPPLIERS

All yarns, including *Jaeger*, supplied by:

Rowan Yarns
Rowan International
Green Lane Mill
Holmfirth
West Yorkshire
HD7 1RW
Tel: 01484 681881
Fax: 01484 687920
E-mail: rowanmail@rowanyarns.co.uk
Website: www.rowanyarns.co.uk
Worldwide distribution. Please phone for details of your nearest stockist

UK
David Morgan Ltd
26 The Hayes
Cardiff
Wales
CF10 1UG
Tel: 029 2022 1011

Stitch Shop
15 The Podium
Northgate
Bath
BA1 5AL
Tel: 01225 481134
Mail order available

Colourway
112A Westbourne Grove
Chepstow Road
London
W2 5RU
Tel/Fax: 020 7229 1432
Mail order available

Liberty plc
214 Regent Street
London W1R 6AH
Tel: 020 7734 1234
Mail order available

Rowan
102 Gloucester Green
Oxford
OX1 2DF
Tel: 01865 793366
Mail order available

Shoreham Knitting & Needlecraft
19 East Street
Shoreham-by-Sea
West Sussex
BN43 5ZE
Tel: 01273 461029
Fax: 01273 465407
E-mail: skn@sure-employ.demon.co.uk
Website: www.englishyarns.co.uk
Mail order available

Bobbins
Wesley Hall
Church Street
Whitby
North Yorkshire
YO22 4DE
Tel/Fax: 01947 600585
E-mail: bobbins@globalnet.co.uk
Mail order available

SOUTH AFRICA
Boldprops (Pty) Ltd
176 Ohrtmann Road
Willowtown
Pietermaritzburg
Tel: 033 76 871

Brooklyn Wool Shop
Duncan Street
Pretoria
Tel: 012 464 504

Creative Kit Company
PO Box 92043
Norwood 2117
Tel: 011 640 6722 / 083 331 7260
Mail order only

Derlee Knitting Mills (Pty) Ltd
Jankelows Building
Jeppestown
Gauteng
Tel: 011 614 6038

Knitting Wool Centre (Pty) Ltd
122 Victoria Road
Woodstock
Cape Town
Tel: 021 447 1134

Swansdon Knitting Wools (Pty) Ltd
8 Foundry Lane
Durban
Tel: 031 304 0488

United Wool (Pty) Ltd
32 Mangold Street
Newton Park
Port Elizabeth
Tel: 041 35 0732

The Wool Shop
Mantle Street
Bloemfontein
Tel: 051 357 4499

AUSTRALIA
Greta's Handcraft Centre
321 Pacific Highway
Lindfield
NSW 2070
Tel: 02 9416 2489
Carry a large range of Rowan Yarns and can give further information on stockists

Knitters of Australia
498 Hampton Street
Hampton
VIC 3188
Tel: 03 9533 1233

Lincraft
Gallery level
Imperial Arcade
Pitt Street
Sydney
New South Wales 2000
Tel: 02 9221 5111
Stores nationwide

Sunspun
185 Canterbury Road
Canterbury
VIC 3126
Tel: 03 9830 1609
Mail order
Distribute and carry a large range of Rowan Yarns and can give further information on stockists

NEW ZEALAND
Knit World
Outlets nationwide
Auckland: 09 837 6111
Tauranga: 07 577 0797
Hastings: 06 878 0090
New Plymouth: 06 758 3171
Palmerston North: 06 356 8974
Wellington: 04 385 1918
Christchurch: 03 379 2300
Dunedin: 03 477 0400
Selected branches stock Rowan wools

Woolmart Wools
Branches throughout South Island and Auckland
Check listings in your local White or Yellow Pages under 'Knitting Wool'

Useful website:
www.thewoolcompany.com

INDEX

Baby blanket 116
Bag 112
Basic fabrics 15
Basic information 17
Basic stitches 10
Blankets 100, 116
Bodywarmer 48
Booties 40, 44, 60
Cables 16
Cardigans 60, 68, 84
Casting off 12
Casting on 9
Decreasing 14

Dog 108
Embroidered moss stitch jacket and booties 44
Embroidery stitches 18
Fair Isle jacket 64
Fair Isle twinset 68
Garter stitch striped jumper, hat and booties 40
Guernseys 32
Hats 36, 40, 92, 112
Heart, star and moon blanket 100
Hooded moss stitch jacket 72
House, heart and flower jacket and hat 36
Increasing 12

Introduction 6
Jacket with lace edging 52
Jacket, trousers, shorts and shoes 22
Jackets 22, 28, 36, 44, 52, 64, 72, 88, 92
Jumpers 40, 68
Lacy shawl 104
Moss stitch cardigan with cable edging 84
Nautical jacket and socks 88
Picot edge cardigan and booties 60
Rabbit family 120
Romper suit 56
Sampler sweater 80
Scandinavian jacket and hat 92
Shawl 104

Shoes 22
Short bolero jacket 28
Shorts 22
Socks 68
Striped bag and hat 112
Striped romper suit 56
Striped tunic 76
Sweater 80
Techniques 8
Three-in-one guernseys 32
Top 96
Toy dog 108
Trousers 22
Tunic 76
Wrap-over top 96

ACKNOWLEDGEMENTS

Thank you to my mother, Norah McTague for inspiring me to knit my first teddy sweater on a holiday in Scotland many, many years ago; to Moira McTague, my sister, for her beautiful illustrations and her ongoing moral and artistic support; and a big thank you to Lucy and Molly, my daughters, for their enthusiasm.
Thanks to all at Rowan Yarns, especially to Stephen Sheard, Kathleen Hargreaves, Elizabeth Armitage and Lyndsey Kaye for their assistance and for delivering the yarn so promptly. Many thanks to Tina Egleton for making my rabbit family and dog come alive, to Sue Whiting for checking all of the patterns, John Freeman for his photography and Frances de Rees, the designer. I would also like to thank the following for their invaluable help: Audrey Athendon, Pat Church, Rae Fraser, Penny Hill, Francis Wallis and Linda Wood. Finally, thanks to Rosemary Wilkinson for making this book possible.